THOROUGHBRED PEDIGREES SIMPLIFIED

MILES NAPIER

This edition published in 2009 by Raceform
Compton, Newbury, Berkshire, RG20 6NL

First published in 1973 by J A Allen & Company Ltd
Revised edition published in 1998 by Langley House Publishing

A catalogue record for this book is available from the British Library.

ISBN 978-1-906820-31-2

Designed by Fiona Pike
Printed in the UK by CPI William Clowes Beccles NR34 7TL

Photographs – *front:* Sadler's Wells with his sons Galileo, Montjeu and High Chaparral; *back:*
Sea The Stars wins the 2009 Eclipse from Rip Van Winkle. Copyright © Edward Whitaker/
Racing Post.

CONTENTS

INTRODUCTION

It has been said that the study of Thoroughbred pedigrees is not very different from – say – that of theology or economics. It is ultimately all a question of faith.

Joking apart, breeding a racehorse involves the marriage of many different parameters: conformational studies; veterinary medical aspects; commercial appeal of the product; logistics; finance – not necessarily in that order.

In addition to the above, a knowledge of Thoroughbred pedigrees is naturally advantageous not only to the breeder, but also to the purchaser and eventual racehorse owner, as well as all others involved with racing on a professional or amateur basis.

Miles Napier's *Thoroughbred Pedigrees Simplified* provides an excellent introduction to its subject for the enthusiastic newcomer, as well as a useful refresher course for the already committed. I thoroughly commend it to all such readers.

Kirsten Rausing
Chairman,
Thoroughbred Breeders' Association

CHAPTER 1:

WHAT IS A PEDIGREE?

The *Concise Oxford Dictionary* defines a pedigree in the following ways: a Genealogical Table; an Ancestral Line of a Man or Animal; the Possession of Ancient Descent; or a Known Line of Descent. The word pedigree is derived from the old French *Pied de Grue*, or Crane's Foot, a mark which denotes succession. Heredity (and thus pedigrees) plays an important part in modern racing and thoroughbred breeding.

The most extensive practical use to which pedigrees are put in modern times is as the components of bloodstock sales catalogues; the tabulated ancestry of each horse entered in the sale is traced back to the third generation, and abbreviated details are given of the racing and breeding records of the first three mares in the direct line of female descent.

Pedigrees also feature in publications devoted to stallions at stud, for example the *Stallion Book*, which is published annually by Weatherbys, the secretariat to the British Horseracing Authority and the Jockey Club and the overall governing body of the thoroughbred breeding industries of both Great Britain and Northern Ireland. Specialist bloodstock and racing publications such as *Thoroughbred Owner And Breeder* (incorporating *Pacemaker*) record the pedigrees of Pattern or Listed (Prestige) races, which are often traced back to five generations.

Pedigrees are produced in large numbers by bloodstock agencies. These are done in relation to stallions which the agencies are promoting or syndicating and to the categories of bloodstock which are on their offer books. Agencies will also produce private pedigrees, stud books and stud cards at the request of individual owners or breeders. These are normally provided for record purposes.

The reason why pedigrees are so important to racing is that without some knowledge of a horse's parents, grandparents and great grandparents it is impossible to make any accurate estimates about that horse's characteristics. A trainer is better placed to map out the future programme of a yearling newly arrived in his yard if he can deduce whether that yearling is likely to mature early or late; to be a fast horse or a stayer (better suited to longer distances); to be placid or temperamental; or to prefer firm or soft going. The owner or manager of a stud needs to possess a working knowledge of pedigrees if he is to plan the matings of the stud's mares in a sensible way; and the same applies to a bloodstock agent or an executive of a bloodstock sales company. Even on the level of finding winners, heredity has a part to play.

Every racing writer should, therefore, have an adequate knowledge of pedigrees. This significance can be explained by the definition of heredity as "the tendency of like to get like" – in other words the tendency for offspring to resemble their parents. In a thoroughbred racehorse this similarity will manifest itself in racecourse performance, colour, conformation or temperament. The great majority of the winners of the most important contests in the history of racing have been the progeny of stallions who were themselves possessed of top-class racing ability. There are, however, notable exceptions to this rule, in particular the now deceased Fairy King, who broke a sesamoid bone in the only race in which he ran, but who became a successful sire of winners.

In order to provide an example of a pedigree of a thoroughbred horse, I have traced the ancestry (to the fifth generation) of Sadler's Wells (incidentally a full brother to Fairy King), who was a really top-class racehorse, and who, although now retired from stud duties, was arguably the outstanding sire of the twentieth century. The influence of Sadler's Wells is likely to continue for many generations to come. Sadler's Wells is a bay horse foaled in the United States of America in 1981.

His sire (father) is Northern Dancer (in racing parlance he is by Northern Dancer). His dam (mother) is Fairy Bridge (he is **out of** Fairy Bridge), who is alternatively described as his first dam. Fairy Bridge is by Bold Reason

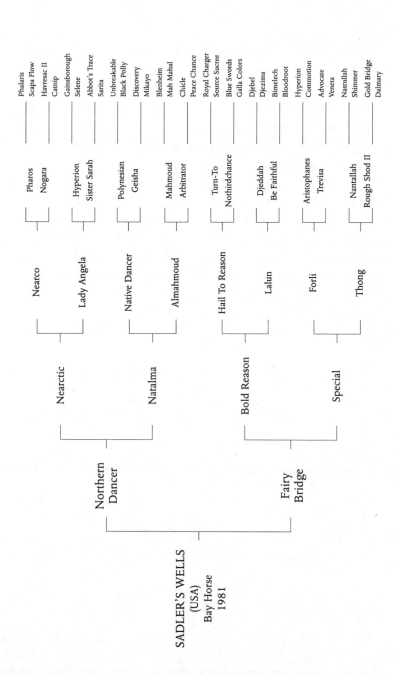

SADLER'S WELLS
(USA)
Bay Horse
1981

Northern Dancer

Fairy Bridge

Nearctic

Natalma

Bold Reason

Special

Nearco

Lady Angela

Native Dancer

Almahmoud

Hail To Reason

Lalun

Forli

Thong

Pharos
Nogara
Hyperion
Sister Sarah
Polynesian
Geisha
Mahmoud
Arbitrator
Turn-To
Nothirdchance
Djeddah
Be Faithful
Aristophanes
Trevisa
Nantallah
Rough Shod II

Phalaris
Scapa Flow
Havresac II
Catnip
Gainsborough
Selene
Abbot's Trace
Sarita
Unbreakable
Black Polly
Discovery
Mikayo
Blenheim
Mah Mahal
Chicle
Peace Chance
Royal Charger
Source Sucree
Blue Swords
Galla Colors
Djebel
Djezima
Bimelech
Bloodroot
Hyperion
Commotion
Advocate
Veneta
Nasrullah
Shimmer
Gold Bridge
Dalmary

and is out of Special, who is therefore the **grandam** (or second dam) of Sadler's Wells. Special is by Forli out of Thong (thus the great grandam – or third dam – of Sadler's Wells).

The dam of Thong is Rough Shod II, who is therefore the great-great grandam, or *fourth* dam of the subject horse, whilst Dalmary is the great-great-great grandam, or *fifth* dam of Sadler's Wells. It will be noticed that the mares in the direct line of female descent appear at the lowest level of the pedigree. This chain of descent is therefore often referred to as the "tail-female" or "bottom" line.

A modern day school of thought maintains that the more remote generations of a horse's ancestry are of limited importance. This attitude, if too rigidly adhered to, can be erroneous. The breeding of thoroughbreds has been a continuous process for 300 years, based on the same principles of heredity. By studying the methods used, it is possible to discover evidence of those principles in action.

CHAPTER 2:

HOW TO COMPILE
A PEDIGREE

The most striking point that is evident from the perusal of a bloodstock sales catalogue is the very strong emphasis that is placed on the "tail-female" or direct line of female descent of all the horses on offer. This will cause any person to wonder why so much more attention should be paid to the "bottom" line than to any other chain of descent in the pedigree.

The importance of the female element in the pedigree of the thoroughbred is a subject that will be dealt with at greater length in Chapter 5. From the commercial point of view the reason why attention is focused so strongly upon the tail-female line is that it is likely to be the weakest chain of descent in the pedigree. Very few stallions who lacked top class racing ability are used extensively at stud; in consequence (provided a horse is reasonably well bred) the merit of the stallions in a pedigree is vouched for by the fact that they are there. The same applies to the dams, grandams and great grandams of these stallions, regardless of their own racing merit.

Racing merit is less important to a mare than it is to a stallion. In the majority of cases the sire in a pedigree will be a better racehorse than the dam, the two grandsires better racehorses than the two mares in the second generation, etc. The male line of descent, which represents generations of selection, is liable to be the strongest chain in the pedigree; the female line of descent is deemed to be the weakest. This is why it needs to be examined in great detail. From the purely Genetic (Hereditary) point of view, the dam of the sire is no less important than the grandam, the three mares in the third generation no less important that the third dam. From the sales point of view the "tail-female" line is the one that matters.

Modern technology has transformed the way in which pedigrees are produced. Where they were once compiled by hand, today they are accessed from the databases of computers. But the basic principles of heredity have not changed; in consequence the ingredients of a sales catalogue remain the same. A brief summary is given of the Racing Records of each of the first three mares in the direct line of female descent regardless of whether those mares won, raced without being placed or never raced at all. If a broodmare is on offer, all her living produce are recorded, together with their name, sex and year of foaling. In the case of all other categories of bloodstock, i.e. yearlings, foals and colts and fillies in and out of training, the dam's full breeding record will be given.

These particulars can be obtained from the *General Stud Book* (see chapter 7) or, in the case of a horse who is not a thoroughbred, from the *Register of Non Thoroughbred Horses*. Details are then recorded of all offspring who won on the Flat, over hurdles or over fences in Great Britain, Ireland or overseas; all offspring who were placed in Great Britain or Ireland; all fillies who became dams of winners in Great Britain, Ireland and overseas – regardless of their own racing records *(together with any British, Irish and foreign winners of any distinction amongst their more remote descendants)*.

The same procedure must be followed for the second and third dams, although their produce will not be recorded in the same detail as is the case with the first dam. If the family in question is particularly strong, the catalogue may confine itself to mentioning only the more important winners.

This information is obtained from the *Statistical Record* which is published annually by Weatherbys. It will be noticed that some of the mares and some of their produce will be recorded in black type and block capitals. These horses are winners of Pattern or Listed (Prestige) races and they are recorded in this way to distinguish them from the winners of unimportant races. Horses who were placed in "Stakes" races, as Pattern or Listed races are sometimes referred to, appear in black type and upper and lower case, whether or not they managed to win. Winners of unimportant races appear in block capitals and light type: horses who were placed and fillies and mares who bred winning offspring are recorded in upper and lower case in light type. In the case of the latter, mention is always made of more remote descendants who won **"black type"** (Prestige) races.

The above paragraphs provide a brief outline of the ingredients of a pedigree. The following example of details from a Tattersalls catalogue has been included to illustrate the method of pedigree compilation.

CHAPTER 3:

A COMMERCIAL PEDIGREE

During the nineteenth century the vast majority of the big studs were owned by private breeders, whose policy was to race the produce themselves. Today most studs, with a few exceptions such as those owned by the Aga Khan and the Maktoum brothers, can only survive economically by operating on a commercial basis – in other words by selling the produce rather than racing them. The policy of most breeders must therefore be to satisfy the demands of the market.

There are two main kinds of "commercial" proposition amongst the young stock. One is the yearling bred for Flat racing, sired by a stallion who is in favour with the buyers and is likely to give those purchasers a quick return on their money by winning as a two-year-old. The other is the jumping-bred store of four or five years old. A jumper begins his racing life later than does a Flat-race horse, which is why the market for jumping-bred yearlings is less strong than that for those bred to race on the Flat. It is a different story however when a horse with a jumping pedigree approaches the age when he can be put into training.

To illustrate the way in which catalogue details are laid out I have taken the example of a yearling, consigned at a Tattersalls October Sale. The yearling is a chestnut filly, foaled on February 27th, 2008, the first foal of her dam. The suffix (GB) after her name denotes that she was foaled in Great Britain. The filly is by Beat Hollow out of Tipsy Me, who was foaled in 2003. The top half of the tabulated pedigree denotes the parents and grandparents of the filly's sire.

Will Stand at Park Paddocks, Somerville Paddock R, Box 349

64 (WITH VAT)
A CHESTNUT FILLY (GB)
Foaled
February 27th, 2008
(first foal)

Beat Hollow (GB)	Sadler's Wells (USA)	Northern Dancer / Fairy Bridge (USA)
	Wemyss Bight (GB)	Dancing Brave (USA) / Bahamian
Tipsy Me (GB) (2003)	Selkirk (USA)	Sharpen Up / Annie Edge
	Time Saved (GB)	Green Desert (USA) / Time Charter

E.B.F. Nominated.

1st Dam
TIPSY ME (GB), placed 3 times at 3 years.

2nd Dam
TIME SAVED (GB), **won** 1 race at 3 years; Own sister to **Illusion (GB)**;
dam of **three winners** from 4 runners and 5 foals of racing age viz
   PLEA BARGAIN (GB) (c. by Machiavellian (USA)), won 3 races at 2 and 3 years and £127,855 including King Edward VII Stakes, York, **Gr.2**, placed second in Prix Greffulhe, Saint-Cloud, **Gr.2**.
   Dubai Time (GB) (c. by Dubai Destination (USA)), won 1 race at 2 years and £6906 and placed twice; also placed once at 2 years in France and £12,728 viz second in Prix des Chenes, Longchamp, **Gr.3**.
   EMIRATES SPORTS (GB), won 1 race at 2 years, 2008, placed once, all his starts.

3rd Dam
TIME CHARTER, Champion older mare in England in 1983, **won** 9 races at home and in France including Champion Stakes, Newmarket, **Gr.1**, Coronation Cup, Epsom, **Gr.1**, King George VI & Queen Elizabeth Stakes, Ascot, **Gr.1**, Oaks, Epsom, **Gr.1**, Sun Chariot Stakes, Newmarket, **Gr.2**, Prix Foy, Longchamp, **Gr.3**, second in Coral Eclipse Stakes, Sandown, **Gr.1**, 1000 Guineas, Newmarket, **Gr.1**, Nassau Stakes, Goodwood, **Gr.2**, Jockey Club Stakes, Newmarket, **Gr.3**, fourth in King George VI & Queen Elizabeth Stakes, **Gr.1** and Prix de l'Arc de Triomphe, Longchamp, **Gr.1**;
dam of **seven winners** from 8 runners and 11 foals of racing age including
   ZINAAD (GB), won 3 races including Jockey Club Stakes, Newmarket, **Gr.2** and Godolphin Stakes, Newmarket, **L.**, second in Henry II Stakes, Sandown, **Gr.3**, third in Prix Kergorlay, Deauville, **Gr.2**, Jockey Club Cup, Newmarket, **Gr.3**, Ormonde EBF Stakes, Chester, **Gr.3**, St Simon Stakes, Newbury, **Gr.3**; sire.
   TIME ALLOWED (GB), won 3 races at 3 and 4 years including Jockey Club Stakes, Newmarket, **Gr.2** and Princess Royal Stakes, Ascot, **Gr.3**, placed second in Park Hill Stakes, Doncaster, **Gr.3**, Galtres Stakes, York, **L.**
   Generous Terms (GB), won 2 races at 3 years, second in March Stakes, **L.**
   Illusion (GB), won 1 race at 3 years, third in Darley Stakes, Newmarket, **L.**
   By Charter, won 1 race at 2 years and placed twice viz second in Cheshire Oaks, Chester, **L.** and third in Fred Archer Stakes, Newmarket, **L.**; dam of winners.
      FIRST CHARTER (GB), 6 races at 3 to 5 years including Weatherbys Insurance Lonsdale Stakes, York, **Gr.2**, placed third in Irish St Leger, **Gr.1**.
      ANTON CHEKHOV (GB), 2 races at home and in France including Prix Hocquart, Longchamp, **Gr.2**, third in Deutsches Derby, Hamburg, **Gr.1**.
      PRIVATE CHARTER (GB), 2 races including Fishpools Furnishings Godolphin Stakes, Newmarket, **L.**, second in Derby Italiano, Rome, **Gr.1**.
      Ridge Runner (GB), 1 race at 2 years; also 8 races in U.S.A. and placed second in Cherokee Run Handicap, Churchill Downs, **L.**
      Careful Timing (GB), 1 race at 3 years, third in Harvest Stakes, Ascot, **L.**
      GREEN CHARTER (GB), 1 race at 2 years; dam of **Perks (IRE)**, 3 races at 3 years, 2008, third in Doonside Cup, Ayr, **L.**, **Safe Trip (GB)**, 1 race at 2 years, second in Coolmore Matchmaker Stakes, Taby, **L.**
      Sharp Terms (GB), unraced; dam of **Sunsemperchi (GB)**, 2 races at 3 and 4 years in Italy, second in Premio Mario Incisa della Rocchetta, Milan, **Gr.3**.
   Not Before Time (IRE), unraced; dam of winners.
      TIME AWAY (IRE), 2 races including Tattersalls Musidora Stakes, York, **Gr.3**, third in Vodafone Nassau Stakes, Goodwood, **Gr.1** and Prix de Diane Hermes, Chantilly, **Gr.1**; dam of **TIME ON (GB)**, 3 races at home and in France including Prix de Malleret, Saint-Cloud, **Gr.2**.
      Time Ahead (GB), 1 race at 3 years and placed twice; also placed once at 3 years in France viz second in Prix de Diane Hermes, Chantilly, **Gr.1**.

Tipsy Me, who was placed three times at three years, is out of Time Saved, who won one race at three years. Time Saved is an own (or full) sister to Illusion, who won a minor race, but was placed in a listed race, and therefore is recorded in upper and lower case and black type. Time Saved, the grandam of the yearling in question, is the dam of three winners, the most successful of whom was Plea Bargain (who is by Machiavellian), who won three races and £127,855 in win and place money, his principal success coming in the King Edward VII Stakes (run that year at York), which is a Group 2 Pattern race. Plea Bargain is therefore, recorded in capitals and black type. Time Saved is also the dam of Dubai Time, the winner of a minor race at two years who also ran second in a Group 2 race and therefore appears in Upper and Lower and black type. The third winner out of Time Saved is Emirates Sports, the winner of a minor race at two years, the only year in which he ran. He appears in capitals in light type.

The third dam (or great granddam) of the yearling filly is Time Charter, the champion older mare in England in 1983, whose four wins at Group 1 level included the Oaks. Time Charter is the dam of two pattern race winners in Zinaad (also a sire) and Time Allowed and of the stakes-placed winners Illusion, Generous Terms and By Charter. Through By Charter, Time Charter is the grandam of three more "black type" winners in First Charter, Anton Chekov and Private Charter; and of a further "black type" winner in Time Away, who is out of Not Before Time, who was unraced and therefore appears in upper and lower and light type.

The present method of cataloguing was first introduced in 1972. It was modelled on the style that had been standard in the catalogues of bloodstock sales in North America – a style which set out to highlight the top class material in a pedigree. The styles that had been in use in English and Irish Catalogues before 1972 had not always been coherent. The relationships between members of the family tended to read in a confusing manner; there was no discrimination between a really high-class racehorse who had won the Derby or a race of similar standing and the winner of a moderate race at a minor meeting; and many vendors sought to disguise weak pedigrees by inserting data that was irrelevant. Other vendors went to the opposite extreme and, by failing to produce adequate family details, did themselves a disservice.

The new method of cataloguing brought about greater uniformity and certainly sorted out the "wheat" from the "chaff." It has to be remembered however that different buyers will look for different information. The buyer of a filly, whether she is a yearling, is in training or out of training, will always think in terms of that filly's eventual prospects at stud. Every winner in the family is important, even a yearling that realises a high sale price needs to be taken into account. Behind this reasoning lies the realisation that the value of a mare or filly can increase considerably overnight through her becoming the dam, half-sister or close relative of the winner of a Prestige race.

Such information, however, is of no interest to the buyer who is searching for a four-year old to put into training over hurdles and who may in future make a steeplechaser. Buyers in this category are more interested in any members of the family who are winners of jumping races – pedigree material, which is, however, viewed with disfavour by prospective buyers of yearlings to race on the Flat (whether colts or fillies). The winners of races over obstacles are normally late-developing horses, and their presence in a pedigree does little to inspire confidence in a yearling buyer hoping to secure a quick return on his money through success in two-year-old races.

Previously catalogue particulars were supplied by different organisations, for instance by the pedigree departments of bloodstock agencies. Today they are normally supplied to the sales companies under contract. For example the pedigrees in the Tattersalls sales catalogues are supplied by Eclipse Pedigrees, which is owned by Weatherbys.

CHAPTER 4:

THE PEDIGREE –
THE MALE LINE

The thoroughbred horse is the outcome in the first instance of crossing the native-bred horses, or Galloways, with the horses of Eastern blood which were imported into England and Ireland during the sixteenth, seventeenth and eighteenth centuries. These horses were indiscriminately referred to as Arabs, Barbs or Turks and named after the persons who owned them at any given moment in time. Racing historians differ as to which of the two breeds was the faster. Some attribute all the good qualities in the modern thoroughbred to Eastern blood; others maintain that the imported Eastern horses "made a very poor showing" when raced against the native breeds. The unsystematic early methods of recording pedigrees leave large areas of doubt over which school of thought was right. What is certain is that the outcome of crossing the Galloways with the Eastern-bred horses was an animal vastly superior to either.

The modern definition of a thoroughbred is "a horse who is in the General Stud Book" (see chapter 7). There is evidence, however, that the term "thoroughbred" was in use some decades before the appearance of the first volume of the above publication. Again there is a division of opinion as to what the term meant. One school of thought suspects that the word was derived from the Arabic word "Kehilan" or pure-bred, and that it is attributable to horses of Arab blood. The rival opinion is that the term was applied to the Galloways, who were themselves a pure breed. However what is clear is that by the end of the nineteenth century the racehorse had become removed from the pure-bred Arab horse by several generations and had developed into a far larger and faster type of horse.

All modern thoroughbreds are descended in direct line of male descent from one of three Arabian horses imported into England in the sixteenth, seventeenth and eighteenth centuries – the Darley Arabian; the Godolphin Arabian (or as he was sometimes known, the Godolphin Barb); and the Byerley Turk. The only other Eastern stallion of importance in modern pedigrees is the Alcock Arabian, who, although extinct in the male line, is the ancestor of every present day grey thoroughbred.

All the three founding stallions owe the survival of their lines to one descendant. The Darley Arabian to his great great grandson Eclipse; the Godolphin Arabian to his grandson Matchem; the Byerley Turk to his great great grandson Herod. The lines are consequently known as the Eclipse, Matchem and Herod lines. The line from Eclipse is by far the strongest; both the Matchem and Herod lines are undergoing a struggle for survival.

The North American sire Northern Dancer brought about a revolution in international thoroughbred breeding. So great was his superiority (and that of his sons and grandsons) over their contemporaries at stud, that many male lines which, twenty years ago, had looked to be in a strong position, have either failed to survive in top-class racing or are in grave danger of collapse. This summary of the sire lines will therefore confine itself to those lines which have a realistic chance of survival.

THE GODOLPHIN ARABIAN
(see page 21)

The Godolphin Arabian is believed to have been of the Jilfan blood of the Yemen and to have been exported via Syria to the stud of the Bey of Tunis. A very savage tempered horse, he is also believed to have been one of four Arab horses presented by the Bey to the King of France, who later sold him to Mr. Edward Coke of Longford Hall, Derbyshire. He was bequeathed to Mr Coke's nephew Lord Godolphin, and it is recorded that he was first used as a teaser to Hobgoblin, the stud's resident stallion. When Hobgoblin refused to cover Roxana, the Godolphin Arabian had the chance to take his place. The outcome in the first instance was the successful racehorse and sire Lath; and in the second Cade, who was a less successful racehorse, but who helped to perpetuate the dynasty.

The line of Cade comes down through Matchem, Conductor, Sorcerer, Comus, a winner of ten races, Humphrey Clinker and Melbourne, who covered at ten guineas a mare at the Rose and Crown at Beverley, to West Australian, the first horse ever to win the three races which constitute the Triple Crown – the 2000 Guineas, the Derby and the St Leger. Melbourne was also the sire of Blink Bonny, the first filly to win both the Derby and the Oaks.

Two branches of the Matchem line survived into the twentieth century and both came down through sons of West Australian. The English line, which was founded by Solon, has now gone under and the one line that did survive, which was founded by Australian, is purely American, although attempts have been made to revive it in Europe.

Australian, who was originally named Millington, was exported to America from Ireland. He was a moderate racehorse, winning only twice, but he was bought to stand at the Woodburn Stud, which housed the famous stallion Lexington – and this was the reason why he received better opportunities than most horses of his racing ability would have done. He became the sire of Spendthrift, the winner of the Belmont Stakes (one of the three races which constitute the American Triple Crown), the sire of Hastings, a good racehorse but possessed of a fiendish temper, whose son, Fair Play, became the sire of Man O'War.

Known affectionately as "Big Red", Man O'War was to become arguably the most famous of all American racehorses. He ran 21 times, suffering defeat only once and winning all his other races – including two American 'Triple Crown' races, the Preakness and Belmont Stakes – without difficulty. Man O'War's son, War Admiral, was the winner of all three of the American Triple Crown races.

The principal representative of the Man O'War line in Europe in recent years was Warning (now dead), the Champion two-year-old of his year and the champion miler at three years. Warning descended from Man O'War through War Relic; Intent, a good stayer of below top-class; Intentionally, a

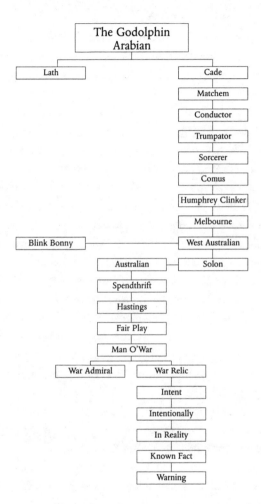

leading two-year-old of his year; In Reality, the winner of the Florida Derby; and Known Fact, the winner of the English 2000 Guineas.

Warning was exported to Japan, where he died in 2000. His most successful sons were Diktat, a Group 1 winner at six and seven furlongs; Piccolo, the winner of the Nunthorpe Stakes (and the sire of La Cucaracha, also a winner of that race); and the Queen Anne Stakes winner Charnwood

Forest. The last-named horse, now dead, is represented at stud by Firebreak, a top-grade international performer. The line is also represented by the European sprint champion Avonbridge, a grandson of Warning through the latter's son Averti.

THE BYERLEY TURK

The Byerley Turk, who was probably an Arabian, is believed to have been obtained by his owner, Captain Robert Byerley, in the battle against the Turks in Hungary. He was later used by his owner, now Colonel Byerley, as a charger during the Battle of the Boyne; the Colonel was then in command of the 6th Dragoon Guards under William of Orange.

Through Jigg, Partner and Tartar, The Byerley Turk became the great great grandsire of Herod (or King Herod as he was first named). Herod, who was bred by the Duke of Cumberland, was a good racehorse, but had weak forelegs and a tendency to break blood vessels.

The most successful of Herod's sons on the racecourse was Highflyer, the unbeaten winner of twelve races and known as "the third great racehorse" (Flying Childers and Eclipse being the first and second to be placed in this category). But, although he was a successful sire of winners, Highflyer did not establish a surviving male line.

Florizel, a further son of Herod, became the sire of Diomed, who won the first ever running of the Derby. Diomed was exported to America and became the direct male line ancestor of Lexington, the most influential sire in North America during the nineteenth century. Lexington, whose male line is extinct, was out of a mare with a very suspect pedigree and became the centre of the controversial Jersey Act (see chapter 7).

None of the British lines from Herod survived into the twentieth century. The two lines that did were both strongly French. These two lines came down through the full-brothers Selim and Castrel, both sons of Buzzard, the winner of twenty-two races and matches who in his turn was by Herod's large, coarse son Woodpecker, who won fourteen races and matches.

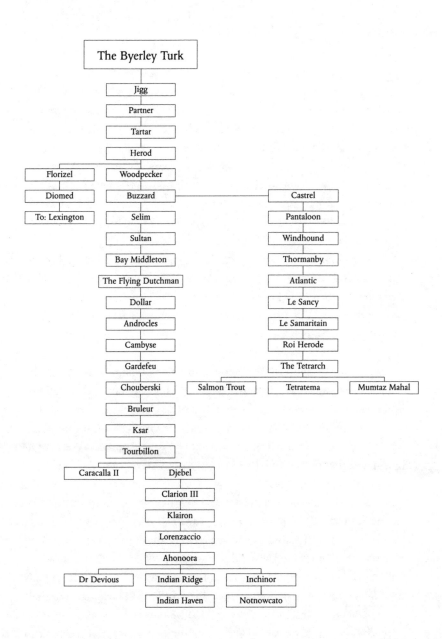

SELIM

Selim was the sire of Sultan, a very good looking horse who was responsible for the unbeaten Bay Middleton, winner of the Derby. Bay Middleton was the sire of an even greater horse in The Flying Dutchman, who won fifteen of his sixteen races. He won the Derby (worth what was then a record sum in prize money), the St Leger and the Ascot Gold Cup, being the first thoroughbred ever to win all three of these races. His only defeat came in the Doncaster Cup, in which he was beaten a neck by the year younger Voltigeur, winner of that year's Derby and St Leger, to whom he was conceding 19lbs. A year later, The Flying Dutchman reversed the form in a return match.

The Flying Dutchman was eventually exported to France where his line came down through Dollar, winner of the Goodwood Cup, Androcles, Cambyse, Gardefeu, winner of the French Derby, Chouberski, Bruleur, winner of the Grand Prix de Paris and the French St Leger, and Ksar, winner of the French Derby and Prix de l'Arc de Triomphe (twice) to Tourbillon.

The winner of the French Derby, Tourbillon, though not out of the ordinary in terms of racing ability, was arguably the most influential sire in the history of French thoroughbred breeding. He was in the top four in the French sires' list for eleven consecutive years, heading the list on four occasions. However the early years of his stud career were marred by the fact that he possessed a high concentration of American blood on the distaff side of his pedigree. This meant that, under the terms of the Jersey Act, which was then in force, neither he nor his progeny could be admitted to the General Stud Book. The "half-bred" stigma which was to be attached to Tourbillon and his descendants was to prove a strong deterrent to British breeders, who did not make as much use of him or his stallion sons as they should have done. However the success of Tourbillon's descendants was to result in the repeal in 1949 of the Jersey Act, and their subsequent admission to the General Stud Book.

Tourbillon's most successful sons were the unbeaten Caracalla II, who won the Grand Prix de Paris and Prix de l'Arc de Triomphe, and Djebel, who won the 2000 Guineas and two runnings of the Prix de l'Arc de Triomphe and was three times champion sire in France. But the line is no longer in so strong a position as it once was. In the past ten years the survival of the Tourbillon line (and indeed the entire male line of Herod) had come to depend on the sprinter Ahonoora (who was destroyed following an injury to an off hind pastern whilst on an out-of-season visit to cover mares in Australia) and his sons. Of the last named Don't Forget Me, the winner of the 2000 Guineas and the Irish 2000 Guineas, was exported to India after a disappointing stud career, whilst the Epsom Derby winner Dr Devious who was exported to Italy, following his repatriation from Japan, did not succeed in siring a top-class son.

It was Indian Ridge, a sprinting son of Ahonoora, who was chiefly instrumental in continuing the male line of Herod. Indian Ridge, a highly successful sire, was based at the Irish National Stud at the time of his death in 2006. His Group 1 winners included that outstanding filly Ridgewood Pearl, who won the Irish 1000 Guineas, the Coronation Stakes, the Breeders' Cup Mile and the Prix du Moulin de Longchamp; Indian Haven, the winner of the Irish 2000 Guineas; Domedriver, the winner of the Breeders' Cup Mile; Indian Ink, the winner of the Coronation Stakes and the top-class sprinters Compton Place and Namid. Indian Haven, Compton Place and Namid have all shown potential as sires.

A further son of Ahonoora to make his mark as a sire was Inchinor, who died in 2003. A very game horse at up to a mile, Inchinor fell just short of top-class as a racehorse. The most successful of his progeny was Notnowcato, successful in the Eclipse Stakes, the Juddmonte International and the Tattersalls Gold Cup, who is now at stud in England. Inchinor was also the sire of Latice, the winner of the French Oaks, Summoner, the winner of the Queen Elizabeth II Stakes and the top-class international sprinter Cape Of Good Hope.

The links in the chain of male descent between Ahonoora and Djebel are provided by Clarion III, a leading two-year-old in France; Klairon, the winner of the French 2000 Guineas; and Lorenzaccio, who defeated the brilliant Nijinsky in the Champion Stakes.

CASTREL

The other line of Herod to come down into the twentieth century came through Castrel, a roarer, Pantaloon, a big chestnut with dark spots, and Windhound to Thormanby, who belonged to Mr. James Merry, a Member of Parliament. Thormanby won 14 races, including the Derby and Ascot Gold Cup and Mr. Merry was subsequently referred to by Mr. Disraeli, the Prime Minister, as "the member for Thormanby." Thormanby sired Atlantic, winner of the 2000 Guineas, who was exported to France, where he sired Le Sancy, the winner of 16 races, sire of Le Samaritain, the sire of Roi Herode.

When Roi Herode was brought over from France to compete in the Doncaster Cup (in which he finished second), the Irish stud owner Mr. Edward Kennedy bought him for the purpose of trying to revive the "lost line of Herod". For a long time it looked as though Mr. Kennedy's ambition would be realised. One of the mares whom Mr. Kennedy sent to Roi Herode was Vahren, a daughter of the 2000 Guineas winner Bona Vista. This unlikely combination of an out and out stayer and the winner of two moderate races was to result in The Tetrarch, possibly the fastest horse of all time.

The Tetrarch created a sensation as the unbeaten winner of seven races as a two-year-old, but during the winter he rapped his off fore fetlock joint and never ran again. He became a great favourite with the public and was nicknamed the "Rocking Horse" because of his spotted grey coat covered with white patches.

Whether The Tetrarch would have proved to be a stayer if he had had the chance to run over long distances will never be known. But he proved to be an influence for stamina (he sired the St Leger winners Caligula, Polemarch and Salmon Trout) as well as speed. He was also the sire of the 2000 Guineas winner Tetratema, as well as the exceptionally fast filly Mumtaz Mahal. Although The Tetrarch was a successful sire of winners, his line did not survive. He has, however, been included in this summary because (principally through Mumtaz Mahal) he has exerted a strong influence on modern breeding.

THE DARLEY ARABIAN

(see pages 28 to 35)

This horse was brought for Mr. James Darley in 1704 by his son who was a merchant in Aleppo. He made his mark quickly as the sire of Flying Childers, the first really great racehorse. Described as "the fleetest horse that ever ran at Newmarket," Flying Childers was never beaten. But it was his own-brother Bartlett's Childers, an animal of no account on the racecourse, who was to perpetuate the line of the Darley Arabian, which came down through Squirt and Marske to Eclipse.

Bred by the Duke of Cumberland, Eclipse was foaled in the same year as the great eclipse of the sun, after which he was named. He did not race until he was five years old and he had so savage a temper that his connections had once seriously thought of having him gelded. But there was no doubt about his excellent ability and an old woman who saw a secret trial swore that "no horse could catch the white-legged one if he ran to the world's end." Eclipse was to win all the 26 races and matches in which he took part, including six King's Plates.

His line survives through his sons Pot-8-Os and King Fergus. The former was so called because a stable lad instead of writing Potato on his box wrote Potoooooooo. He was a tough horse, winning 34 of the 46 races in which he ran. King Fergus was a "horse of great size".

The one line of King Fergus that seemed to have had a realistic chance of survival was the line known as the "St. Simon line." St Simon came down from King Fergus through the St Leger winner Hambletonian, Whitelock, the bad-tempered Blacklock, Voltaire, winner of the Doncaster Cup, Voltigeur, winner of the Derby, St Leger and Doncaster Cup (in the latter race beating The Flying Dutchman); Vedette, winner of the 2000 Guineas and of two Doncaster Cups, and the Derby winner Galopin.

The last-named horse was owned by Prince Batthyany, who was also the breeder of St Simon. When the Prince collapsed and died of a heart attack in the luncheon room of the Jockey Club Stand at Newmarket, St Simon's classic engagements became void. But, in the colours of the Duke of Portland, he won the Epsom Cup, the Goodwood Cup and the

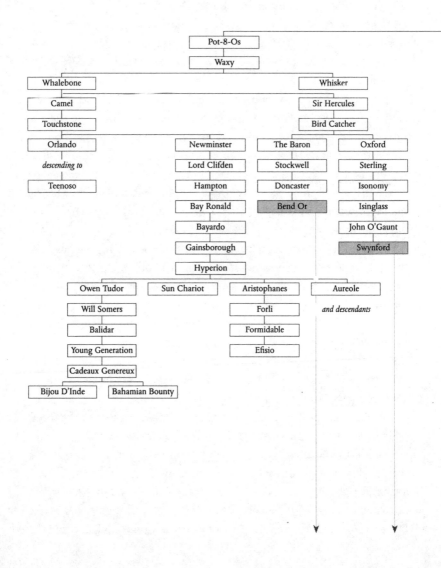

St. Simon Line

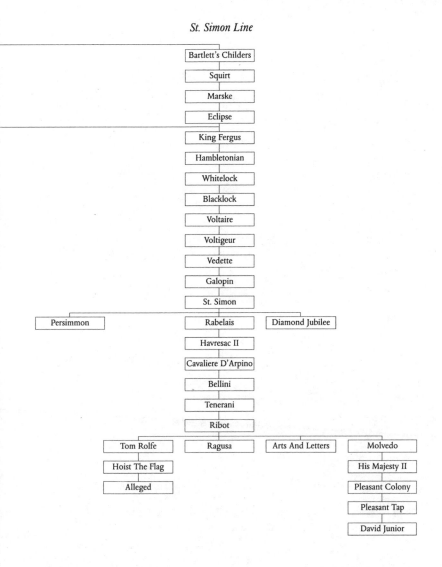

Grey shading denotes male
line continues overleaf

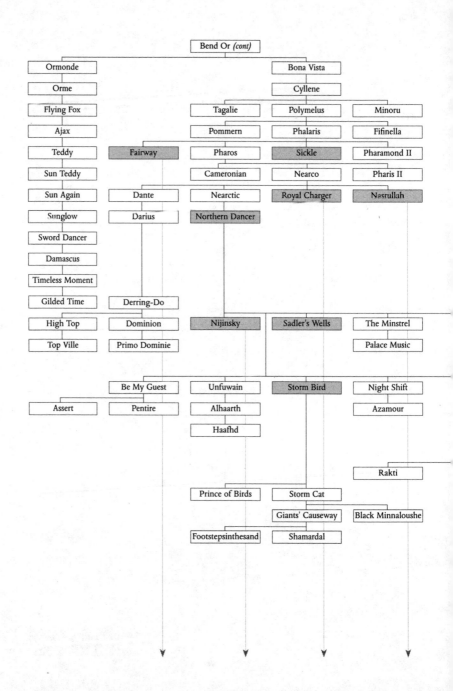

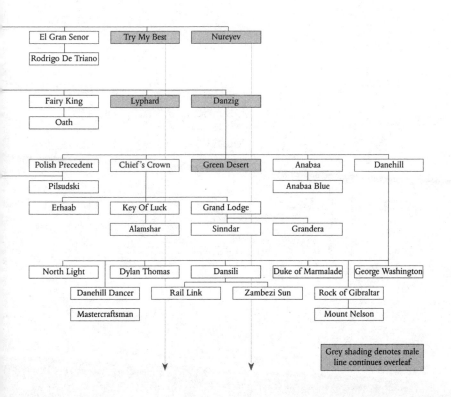

| El Gran Senor | Try My Best | Nureyev |
| Rodrigo De Triano | | |

| Fairy King | Lyphard | Danzig |
| Oath | | |

Polish Precedent	Chief's Crown	Green Desert	Anabaa	Danehill
Pilsudski			Anabaa Blue	
Erhaab	Key Of Luck	Grand Lodge		
	Alamshar	Sinndar	Grandera	

North Light	Dylan Thomas	Dansili	Duke of Marmalade	George Washington
Danehill Dancer	Rail Link	Zambezi Sun	Rock of Gibraltar	
Mastercraftsman			Mount Nelson	

Grey shading denotes male line continues overleaf

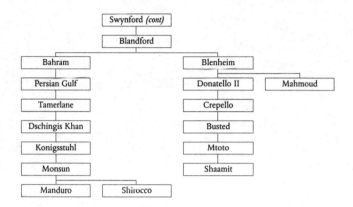

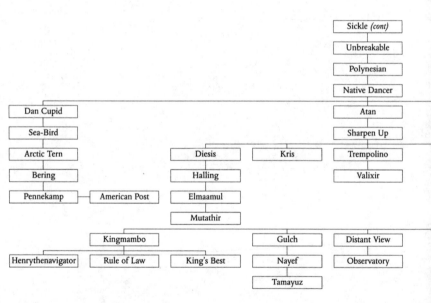

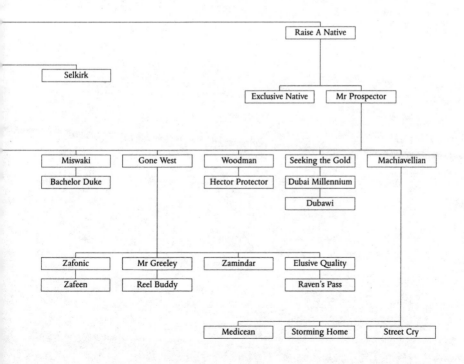

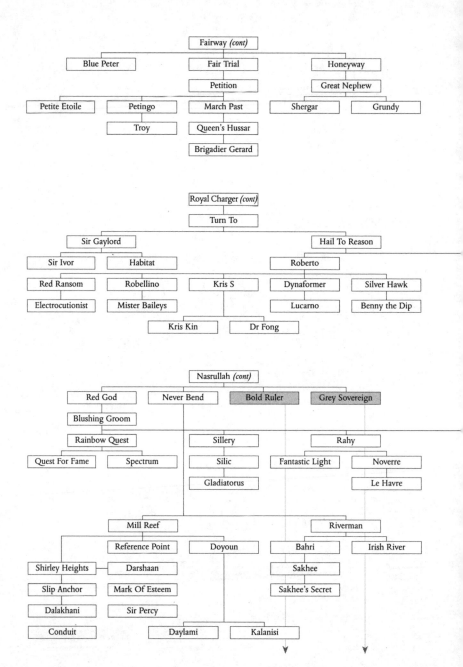

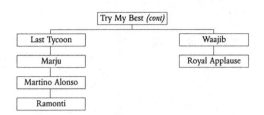

Try My Best *(cont)*

Last Tycoon	Waajib
Marju	Royal Applause
Martino Alonso	
Ramonti	

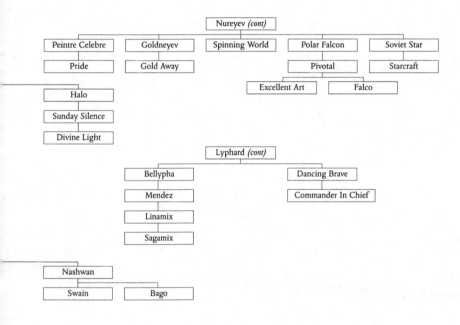

Nureyev *(cont)*

Peintre Celebre	Goldneyev	Spinning World	Polar Falcon	Soviet Star
Pride	Gold Away		Pivotal	Starcraft

Excellent Art	Falco

Halo
Sunday Silence
Divine Light

Lyphard *(cont)*

Bellypha	Dancing Brave
Mendez	Commander In Chief
Linamix	
Sagamix	

Nashwan	
Swain	Bago

Green Desert *(cont)*

Cape Cross	Desert Prince	Desert Style	Oasis Dream	Invincible Spirit
Sea the Stars				Lawman

Bachir	Paco Boy

Grey shading denotes male
line continues overleaf

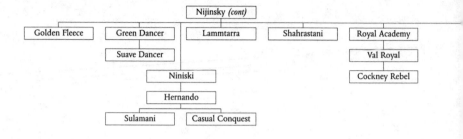

Nijinsky *(cont)*

- Golden Fleece
- Green Dancer
  - Suave Dancer
- Lammtarra
  - Niniski
    - Hernando
      - Sulamani
      - Casual Conquest
- Shahrastani
- Royal Academy
  - Val Royal
    - Cockney Rebel

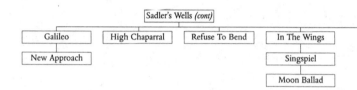

Sadler's Wells *(cont)*

- Galileo
  - New Approach
- High Chaparral
- Refuse To Bend
- In The Wings
  - Singspiel
    - Moon Ballad

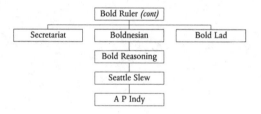

Bold Ruler *(cont)*

- Secretariat
- Boldnesian
  - Bold Reasoning
    - Seattle Slew
      - A P Indy
- Bold Lad

Grey Sovereign *(cont)*

- Zeddaan
  - Kalamoun
    - Kenmare
      - Highest Honor
        - Verglas
          - Silver Frost
- Fortino
  - Caro
    - Mizzen Mast
    - Kaldoun
      - Smadoun
        - Chichicastenango
          - Vision D'Etat

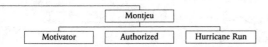

Ascot Gold Cup by 20 lengths. He was never beaten and was undoubtedly one of the greatest racehorses of all time. He was an equally outstanding stallion, heading the sires' list for seven consecutive years and becoming the sire of the winners of 16 English classic races – a feat not matched even by Northern Dancer.

St. Simon's outstanding sons were the own-brothers Persimmon and Diamond Jubilee, both bred and owned by the Prince of Wales (later King Edward VII). The first named won the Derby, St Leger and Ascot Gold Cup; the second, who inherited his sire's temperament in full measure, won the Triple Crown of the 2000 Guineas, Derby and St Leger. St Simon's outstanding daughter was La Fleche, winner of the 1000 Guineas, Oaks, St Leger and Ascot Gold Cup. Persimmon became the sire of Sceptre, the only horse in the history of racing to win four classic races (she won the 2000 Guineas, 1000 Guineas, Oaks and St Leger) and of Prince Palatine, the winner of the St Leger, the Eclipse Stakes and Ascot Gold Cup, twice.

The lines of St Simon that remained extant owed their existence to that horse's great great great great grandson Ribot. This horse's line descends through the temperamental Rabelais, the winner of the Goodwood Cup; Havresac II; Cavaliere d'Arpino, winner of the Milan Grand Prix (and considered by his owner-breeder Federico Tesio to have been the best horse he ever owned), Bellini, winner of the Italian Derby and St Leger; and Tenerani, who won the Italian Derby and the Goodwood Cup and was leased to the English National Stud.

In the opinion of many good judges Ribot was the greatest horse to have raced in the entire history of the Turf. Bred by Signor Federico Tesio, he was the unbeaten winner of 16 races in Italy, France and England, including the King George VI and Queen Elizabeth Stakes and the Prix de l'Arc de Triomphe, twice. Ribot stood his first season at the Woodland Stud at Newmarket, was returned to Italy at the end of the year and three years later was leased to Mr. J.W. Galbreath's Darby Dan Farm in Kentucky for $1,300,000 – remaining in the USA when no satisfactory arrangements could be made for him to return to Italy on the expiry of his lease.

Ribot headed the list of sires in Great Britain and Ireland three times. His most successful sons in Europe were Ragusa, winner of the Irish Sweeps Derby, the St Leger and the King George VI and Queen Elizabeth Stakes; and Molvedo, the winner of the Prix de l'Arc de Triomphe and the Grand Prix de Deauville. In America, Ribot's most successful sons were "Horse of the Year" Arts and Letters, winner of the Belmont Stakes and Tom Rolfe, the winner of the Preakness Stakes.

Although Ragusa was a successful sire of winners, neither he nor Molvedo managed to establish lasting lines. Ribot's great-grandson Alleged, a dual winner of the Prix de l'Arc de Triomphe, has sired the Irish Derby winners Law Society and Sir Harry Lewis and the St Leger winner Shantou. But this line now seems more likely to feature in jump racing than in top-class international Flat racing.

The one representative of the Ribot male line to demonstrate top-class form in Europe in recent years is David Junior, the winner of the Eclipse Stakes and the Champion Stakes, who comes down from Ribot through His Majesty II, Pleasant Colony and the American Champion Pleasant Tap.

POT-8-OS

To return to Pot-8-Os, who founded the stronger of the two extant lines of Eclipse. The former horse was the sire of Champion, the first horse to win both the Derby and the St Leger, and Waxy, the winner of the Derby on his first appearance on a racecourse. From Waxy and Penelope, the winner of 18 races, the Duke of Grafton and his son bred the brothers Whalebone and Whisker, both winners of the Derby.

CAMEL

It was through Whalebone and his sons Camel and Sir Hercules that the Pot-8-Os line of Eclipse has survived. Camel, who was "quartered like a carthorse," was the sire of Touchstone, who won the St Leger, the Doncaster Cup, twice and the Ascot Gold Cup, twice. Three sons of Touchstone won the Derby, including Orlando, who was awarded the race when it was discovered that the horse who passed the post first

"Running Rein" was in fact a four-year-old named Maccabeus. Orlando was exported to the USA where his line survives today largely through the "Black Whirlwind" Domino.

The most successful representative of the line in Europe in modern times was Teenoso, the winner of the Derby and the King George VI and Queen Elizabeth Stakes, who died in 2000.

However the principal "raison d'etre" of the Camel line is the dynasty founded by Hyperion. The links in the chain of descent between Touchstone and Hyperion are the St Leger winner Newminster; his son, Lord Clifden, also a St Leger winner; Hampton, who started life as a selling plater, but went on to win the Goodwood and Doncaster Cups; Bay Ronald, the winner of the Coronation Cup; Bayardo, the winner of the St Leger and the Ascot Gold Cup and probably the outstanding horse to race during the first decade of the twentieth century; and Gainsborough, winner of the Triple Crown of the 2000 Guineas, Derby and St Leger as well as the Ascot Gold Cup.

Hyperion stood only 15 hands and 1½ inches, but was a horse of beautiful quality and one of the finest thoroughbreds of his day both at stud and on the racecourse. He was the winner of the Derby in what was then the record time for the race and also the St Leger. At stud he headed the sires' list on six occasions and was responsible for the winners of eleven classic races. His most successful sons were Owen Tudor, who won a wartime Derby and Gold Cup, and the Queen's Aureole, the winner of the King George VI and Queen Elizabeth Stakes. His most successful daughter was Sun Chariot, the winner of a wartime 1000 Guineas, Oaks and St Leger in the colours of King George VI.

Aureole, although a successful sire of winners, failed to establish a lasting line – and the same is true of his grandson Vaguely Noble, the winner of the Prix de l'Arc de Triomphe.

For all his prowess as a progenitor, there are only two lines of Hyperion which have survived in top-class racing – and these are surviving only marginally. The first comes down through Owen Tudor; his brilliant 2000 Guineas-winning son Tudor Minstrel (rated jointly with Brigadier Gerard as the outstanding miler to race in Great Britain since the war);

Will Somers; Balidar, the champion sprinter in Europe; Young Generation, a leading two-year-old and a top-class three-year-old miler; to the Champion sprinter Cadeaux Genereux, a highly successful sire during the first decade of the 21st century. The latter's Group 1 winners include the St James's Palace Stakes winner Bijou D'Inde and the fast two-year-old Bahamian Bounty, himself a successful sire of sprinters.

The second extant line of Hyperion descends through Aristophanes; Forli, a quadruple crown winner in the Argentine; and the Middle Park Stakes winner Formidable to Efisio, a Group 1 winner in Italy ,who died in 2008. Efisio's most successful progeny were the fillies Attraction, the only horse to win the 1000 Guineas, the Irish 1000 Guineas and the Coronation Stakes; and Pearly Shells, a top-class winner in France. But there exists a possibility that Efisio's top-class international performing son Le Vie Dei Colori may have left a good horse, in spite of his premature death.

SIR HERCULES

The most influential son of Whalebone, however, was Sir Hercules. His son Birdcatcher was responsible for The Baron, the winner of the St Leger and the Cesarewitch, and for Oxford, whose son Sterling sired Isonomy, twice the winner of the Ascot Gold Cup.

OXFORD

Isonomy's son Gallinule (a "roarer") was the sire of Pretty Polly, one of the greatest fillies to race on the turf and the winner of the 1000 Guineas, Oaks and St Leger and narrowly beaten in the Gold Cup. But the horse who was to carry on the line was Isinglass, a superb racehorse who won 11 of the 12 races in which he ran, including the 2000 Guineas, Derby, St Leger and Ascot Gold Cup; Isinglass won more in stake money than any thoroughbred prior to 1952. At Stud, Isinglass was mated with La Fleche and the offspring of this union was John O'Gaunt, a horse who was not really sound, but who ran second in the 2000 Guineas and the Derby. John O'Gaunt became the sire of Swynford, a late developer, but a horse of the highest class and the winner of the St Leger and the Eclipse Stakes.

Swynford's son Blandford, although a mediocre racehorse, became a great sire, and was the progenitor of four winners of the Derby. His greatest son on the racecourse was the unbeaten Bahram, the winner of the Triple Crown of the 2000 Guineas, Derby and St Leger. Bahram achieved some excellent results in the five seasons during which he stood in England. But his English line did not survive and he was not a success as a sire either in the United States, to which country he was exported in 1940, or subsequently in Argentina.

However it was a line from Bahram which had been developed solely in Germany that seems to have come to the rescue of the Swynford line – the branch from Crepello having ceased to be fashionable. The German stallion Monsun, one of the highest rated horses of his generation in Germany, has sprung from relative obscurity to make a major impact on international racing through the successes of Manduro (Prince Of Wales's Stakes, Prix Jacques Le Marois and Prix D'Ispahan) Shirocco (Breeders' Cup Turf and Coronation Cup) and the French Oaks winner Stacelita. The line comes down via Bahram's son Persian Gulf, the winner of the Coronation Cup; Tamerlane, the winner of the St James's Palace Stakes; Dschingis Khan; and Konigsstuhl.

Mtoto (who is now retired from stud duties) had appeared to represent the Blandford line's chief hope of survival following the success of his son Shaamit (later the sire of the St Leger winner Bollin Eric) in the Derby. A very high-class horse, Mtoto won the Eclipse Stakes twice and also the King George VI and Queen Elizabeth Stakes and descends from Blandford through the Derby winner Blenheim; the Italian Derby winner Donatello II; the 2000 Guineas and Derby winner Crepello; and Busted who won the King George VI and Queen Elizabeth Stakes and the Eclipse Stakes.

THE BARON

The Baron (the more influential of Birdcatcher's sons) was to become an important link in the strongest chain of male descent in the history of thoroughbred breeding. The winner of the St Leger and the Cesarewitch, he became the sire of Stockwell, the winner of the 2000 Guineas and the

St Leger. The last-named horse achieved great success at stud, earning himself the sobriquet of "Emperor of Stallions."

He sired three winners of the Derby, including the "Triple Crown" winner Lord Lyon and Doncaster. The latter's son Bend Or, partnered by the champion jockey Fred Archer, defeated Robert The Devil in one of the most desperate finishes ever seen in the Derby. Bend Or was responsible for the 2000 Guineas winner Bona Vista and Ormonde.

ORMONDE

Bred and owned by the Duke of Westminster, Ormonde must rank with St Simon and Isinglass as one of the three great racehorses of the nineteenth century. Although he was a "roarer" and unsound, he was never beaten, winning sixteen races, including the "Triple Crown" and the Champion Stakes. Unfortunately he was a poor breeder to the point of being almost sterile and achieved little when sold, firstly to the Argentine, and later to America. His line, however, was maintained by his son Orme, twice the winner of the Eclipse Stakes. Although this line was once strong, it's most powerful branches have gone under.

The line seems more likely to survive in America than in Europe. The principal representative of the line in America is Gilded Time, the winner of the Breeders' Cup Juvenile. His line comes down through Orme, through the "Triple Crown" winner Flying Fox; through the Grand Prix de Paris winner Ajax; through Teddy, Sun Teddy, Sun Again, Sunglow; Sword Dancer, the winner of the Belmont Stakes to Damascus the "Horse of the Year" and Timeless Moment.

BONA VISTA

Bona Vista was the sire of Cyllene, the winner of nine races, including the Gold Cup and a great stallion, being the sire of four winners of the Derby, including Tagalie, who also won the 1000 Guineas, and Minoru, who also won the 2000 Guineas in the colours of King Edward VII. But it was Polymelus, the winner of the Champion Stakes and five times the leading sire, who carried the line down to modern times. Polymelus sired three winners of the Derby, including the Triple Crown winner Pommern and Fifinella, also winner of the Oaks. Polymelus's son Phalaris, the winner of 16 races, was another outstanding sire. His line is extant today through two sets of full-brothers, Pharos and Fairway, and Sickle and Pharamond II, the latter two of whom were out of Selene, the dam of Hyperion, and both of whom were exported to the United States. Pharos won 14 races including the Champion Stakes and was the sire of Cameronian, winner of the 2000 Guineas and Derby, Pharis II and Nearco. Pharis II, bred and owned by Marcel Boussac, was unbeaten in the three races in which he ran, including the French Derby and the Grand Prix de Paris. Although a very successful sire of winners he did not establish a lasting line.

NEARCO
Nearco, also a brilliant racehorse, was the unbeaten winner of 14 races, including the Grand Prix de Paris. Bred and raced by Senator Federico Tesio, he was bought by Mr Martin Benson for the then world record price of £60,000 and imported into England. He was to become a further potent link in the most powerful male line of today and was twice Champion sire. The sons through whom his lines survive today are the Derby winner Dante, the brilliant but temperamental Nasrullah, Royal Charger, the winner of the Challenge Stakes at Newmarket and Nearctic, the winner of 21 races in Canada and voted Horse of the Year in that country.

NORTHERN DANCER
Nearctic was the sire of Northern Dancer, who, in the opinion of many good judges was the most successful stallion in the history of thoroughbred breeding and the horse who revolutionised the thoroughbred. Northern Dancer was bred in Canada by Mr E. P. Taylor and won 14 races (from 15 starts), including the Preakness Stakes and the Kentucky Derby (in record time). He was four times champion European sire and was, to 2008, the progenitor, grandsire, great grandsire or direct male ancestor of the winners of no fewer than 111 runnings of the five English Classics (the 2000 Guineas, the 1000 Guineas, the Derby, the Oaks and the St

Leger), the Irish Derby and the King George VI and Queen Elizabeth Stakes. His most famous sons were Nijinsky, the first horse since Bahram in 1935 to win the Triple Crown, who also won the Irish Derby and the King George VI and Queen Elizabeth Stakes in the colours of the late Mr Charles Engelhard; The Minstrel, a very close relation of Nijinsky, who won the English and Irish Derbies and the King George VI and Queen Elizabeth Stakes; and El Gran Senor, the winner of the 2000 Guineas and the Irish Derby.

TRY MY BEST

Try My Best, an own-brother to El Gran Senor, has established a potent sprinting line through Waajib, Royal Applause, Acclamation and Equiano.

Last Tycoon, a son of Try My Best, who excelled at sprint and mile distances, is the sire in his turn of Marju, a top-class miler. Marju is the sire of the high-class mare Soviet Song, the winner of five Group 1 races, whilst his son, Martino Alonso is responsible for Ramonti (Sussex Stakes and St James's Palace Stakes).

SADLER'S WELLS

Sadler's Wells proved to be Northern Dancer's outstanding sire son, and in the opinion of many, a rival to his progenitor for the accolade of champion twentieth century sire. The winner of the Irish 2000 Guineas and the Eclipse Stakes, Sadler's Wells headed the sires' list on no fewer than 14 occasions. He was responsible for the Derby winners Galileo (also successful in the Irish Derby and the King George VI and Queen Elizabeth Stakes) and High Chaparral (also the winner of the Irish Derby and the Breeders' Cup Turf, twice). He sired a record number of five winners of the Oaks, including Salsabil (also the winner of the 1000 Guineas and the Irish Derby) and Alexandrova (who went on to win the Yorkshire Oaks). He was the progenitor of three winners of the 2000 Guineas, including Refuse To Bend (also successful in the Eclipse Stakes and the Queen Anne Stakes); of three winners of the St Leger; of the winners of five runnings of the King George VI and Queen Elizabeth Stakes; and of the winners of a record six runnings of the Ascot Gold Cup, including Yeats, who won the race an historic four times.

Galileo is the sire of New Approach (Derby and Champion Stakes), Soldier of Fortune (Irish Derby and Coronation Cup), Lush Lashes (Coronation Stakes and Yorkshire Oaks), Teofilo (unbeaten as a two-year-old), Red Rocks (Breeders' Turf Cup), Sixties Icon (St Leger) and Rip Van Winkle (Sussex Stakes).

Montjeu, one of two sons of Sadler's Wells to win the Prix de l'Arc de Triomphe, was the winner of five additional Group 1 races, including the French and Irish Derbies and the King George VI and Queen Elizabeth Stakes. He has proved to be a most successful stallion. He is the progenitor of the Epsom Derby winners Motivator and Authorized (also the winner of the Juddmonte International Stakes), also of Hurricane Run (Irish Derby, King George VI and Queen Elizabeth Stakes and Prix de l'Arc de Triomphe) of the Irish Derby winners Frozen Fire and Fame And Glory, of Scorpion (St. Leger, Coronation Cup and Grand Prix de Paris) and of Montmartre (Grand Prix de Paris).

The Sadler's Wells horse In the Wings, who won the Breeders' Cup Turf and the Coronation Cup, was the sire of Singspiel, the winner of £3 million in stake money. Singspiel in his turn sired Moon Ballad, the winner of the Dubai World Cup, and Da Re Mi (Yorkshire Oaks).

Nijinksy was responsible for three Epsom Derby winners in Golden Fleece, Shahrastani (who also won the Irish Derby) and Lammtarra, also the winner of the King George VI and Queen Elizabeth Stakes and the Prix de l'Arc de Triomphe. Kahyasi, who won both the English and the Irish Derbies, was a grandson of Nijinsky through Ile de Bourbon, the winner of the King George VI and Queen Elizabeth Stakes. Nijinksy's son Caerleon won the French Derby and sired Generous, winner of the Derby, Irish Derby and King George VI and Queen Elizabeth Stakes, as well as the Oaks winner Lady Carla and the 1000 Guineas winner Cape Verdi.

Royal Academy, Nijinsky's Breeders' Cup Mile-winning son, sired the 1000 Guineas winner Sleepytime and a further Breeders' Cup winner in Val Royal, whose son Cockney Rebel won both the English and Irish

2000 Guineas. Green Dancer, who won the French 2000 Guineas was the sire of Suave Dancer, the winner of the Prix de l'Arc de Triomphe and of the French 2000 Guineas winner Green Tune. Suave Dancer sired the Eclipse Stakes winner Compton Admiral.

The strongest of the lines from Nijinsky comes down through the French St Leger winner Niniski to Hernando, who won the French Derby and sired two winners of that classic in Sulamani (also the winner of another five Group races) and Holding Court. Hernando achieved further fame late in life as the sire of the Oaks winner Look Here and of an additional Group 1 winner in Casual Conquest.

THE MINSTREL

The Minstrel was the sire of the 1000 Guineas winner Musical Bliss and of the Champion Stakes winner Palace Music, the latter becoming the progenitor of the American champion Cigar.

EL GRAN SENOR

El Gran Senor is the sire of Rodrigo de Triano, who won the 2000 Guineas, the Irish 2000 Guineas and the Champion Stakes; and of Belmez, the winner of the King George VI and Queen Elizabeth Stakes.

NUREYEV

This son of Northern Dancer who was the champion miler in Europe, was sadly disqualified after finishing first in the 2000 Guineas. The most successful of his daughters were Miesque (1000 Guineas and Breeders Cup Mile, twice) and Reams Of Verse (Oaks). Although mainly an influence for speed, he sired Peintre Celebre, successful in the French Derby, Grand Prix de Paris and Prix de l'Arc de Triomphe. Peintre Celebre sired the Champion Stakes winner Pride.

Soviet Star was a versatile son of Nureyev, winning the French 2000 Guineas and the Sussex Stakes over a mile and the July Cup over six furlongs. On the racecourse, his most successful sons were Starcraft, the champion miler in Europe and Australia; Soviet Line, twice the winner of the Lockinge Stakes; Starborough, the winner of the St James's Palace Stakes; and Ashkalani, successful in the French 2000 Guineas.

Goldneyev, a near top-class son of Nureyev, was the grandsire, through Gold Away, of an exceptional filly in Alexander Goldrun, who took five Group 1 races.

Spinning World, whose five Group 1 successes included the Irish 2000 Guineas and the Breeders' Cup Mile, is also siring winners in the top-grade.

The most influential of Nureyev's sons is, however, Polar Falcon (a top-class performer from six furlongs to a mile) through his son Pivotal. Although a speedy racehorse and primarily an influence for speed at stud, Pivotal is none the less the sire of Sariska, the winner of the Oaks and the Irish Oaks. Other top-class members of Pivotal's progeny include the French 2000 Guineas winner Falco, the St James's Palace Stakes winner Excellent Art, the Lockinge Stakes winner Peeress, Saoire, the winner of the Irish 1000 Guineas and Halfway To Heaven, who added the Nassau Stakes and Sun Chariot Stakes to her victory in the Irish 1000 Guineas.

STORM BIRD

Storm Bird, the leading two-year-old of his generation, did much to propagate the Northern Dancer line. His most successful progeny on the Flat in Europe were Balanchine (Epsom Oaks and Irish Derby), Indian Skimmer (French Oaks and Champion Stakes) and Prince of Birds (Irish 2000 Guineas). But Storm Cat, a top-class sprinter in the USA, has been the most influential of Storm Bird's sons at stud. The first-named has sired the Irish 2000 Guineas winner Black Minnaloushe, Giant's Causeway, who won the St James's Palace Stakes, the Sussex Stakes, Eclipse Stakes and Irish Champion Stakes; Aljabr, winner of the Lockinge Stakes; and Nebraska Tornado, the winner of the French Oaks. Giant's Causeway has been a successful stallion, his progeny including Footstepsinthesand (2000 Guineas), Ghanaati (1000 Guineas and Coronation Stakes), Shamardal (French 2000 Guineas, French Derby and St James's Palace Stakes) and Maids Causeway (Coronation Stakes).

LYPHARD

Dancing Brave, the brilliant winner of the 2000 Guineas, King George VI and Queen Elizabeth Stakes, Eclipse Stakes and the Prix de l'Arc de Triomphe, was outstanding amongst Lyphard's sons on the racecourse. Commander In Chief, the winner of the English and Irish Derbies, and the Italian Derby winner White Muzzle are sons of Dancing Brave who have been influential in Japan.

In Europe, Linamix has been the most influential of Lyphard's descendants, his line coming down through Bellypha and Mendez. Sagamix, the winner of the Prix de l'Arc de Triomphe and the Grand Prix de Paris winner Slickly are amongst the numerous top class winners which Linamix has sired.

BE MY GUEST

A high-class miler son of Northern Dancer, Be My Guest is responsible for On The House (1000 Guineas and Sussex Stakes), Assert (French and Irish Derbies) and Pentire (King George VI and Queen Elizabeth Stakes).

UNFUWAIN

A high-class middle-distance performer and a half-brother to the outstanding Nashwan, Unfuwain has proved to be an excellent sire of fillies. His daughters included Lahan (1000 Guineas), Eswarah (Oaks), the excellent Petrushka (Irish Oaks and Yorkshire Oaks), two further Irish Oaks winners in Lailani and Bolas and Zahrat Dubai (Nassau Stakes). Unfuwain's son Alhaarth, the champion two-year-old of his year, is the sire of Haafhd (2000 Guineas and Champion Stakes).

There were three sons of Northern Dancer who, whilst undistinguished on the racecourse, proved to be highly successful at stud.

NIGHT SHIFT

The winner of a solitary race over six furlongs, Night Shift nevertheless sired the versatile and high-class Azamour, who won the St James's Palace Stakes, Irish Champion Stakes and King George VI and Queen Elizabeth

Stakes. In the Groove, who took the Irish 1000 Guineas, Champion Stakes and Coronation Cup, and Daryaba, the winner of the French Oaks, were Night Shift's most successful daughters.

FAIRY KING

Fairy King, an own-brother to Sadler's Wells, raced only once. However he was the sire of the Derby winner Oath, Falbrav, the winner of the Eclipse Stakes and the Queen Elizabeth II Stakes, Helissio, who won the Prix de l'Arc de Triomphe and the Grand Prix de Saint Cloud (twice), and Turtle Island, who both won the Irish 2000 Guineas and sired the English 2000 Guineas winner Island Sands.

DANZIG

The winner of three unimportant races, Danzig became a sensational sire of fast horses and a strong influence at stud. He sired six winners of the July Cup (one of the principal sprint races), including the exceptionally fast Dayjur. His most successful winners beyond sprint distances included Polish Precedent, a dual Group 1-winning miler), Ad Valorem (Queen Anne Stakes), Lure (Breeders' Cup Mile) and Astronomer Royal (French 2000 Guineas).

Polish Precedent made his mark at stud as the sire of Pilsudski (successful in six Group 1 races, including the Eclipse Stakes and the English and Irish Champion Stakes). Other top class winners by Polish Precedent included Rakti (Champion Stakes and Queen Elizabeth II Stakes), Court Masterpiece (Sussex Stakes), Pure Grain (Irish Oaks and Yorkshire Oaks) and Darsi (French Derby).

Anabaa, one of Danzig's July-Cup winning sons, went on to become the sire of the excellent filly Goldikova and of the French Derby winner Anabaa Blue.

Chief's Crown was a son of Danzig, who became the champion two-year-old in America. He was the sire of the Epsom Derby winner Erhaab and the grandsire (through the St James's Palace Stakes winner Grand Lodge) of the Aga Khan's Sinndar, a further Epsom Derby winner, also successful in the Irish Derby and the Prix de l'Arc de Triomphe. Sinndar went on to sire the very high-class international campaigner Youmzain and the Irish Oaks winner Shawanda. Grand Lodge also sired the Irish Champion Stakes and Prince Of Wales's Stakes winner Grandera. Key Of Luck, also a son of Chief's Crown, sired Alamshar, successful in the Irish Derby and the King George VI and Queen Elizabeth Stakes.

Although the Danzig horse Green Desert ran second in the 2000 Guineas, he was at his most effective over sprint distances and was the winner of the July Cup. Although principally an influence for speed, he is the sire of the top-class milers Cape Cross (Lockinge Stakes) and Desert Prince (Irish 2000 Guineas and Queen Elizabeth II Stakes). Cape Cross is the sire of two exceptional horses in Ouija Board (Oaks, Irish Oaks, Prince Of Wales' Stakes and Breeders Cup Filly & Mare, twice) and Sea The Stars (2000 Guineas, Derby and Prix de l'Arc de Triomphe).

Other sons of Green Desert to make their mark at stud are Invincible Spirit, Desert Style and Oasis Dream. Midday, a daughter of the last-named, won the Nassau Stakes. Invincible Spirit, top class at sprint distances, sired Lawman, who stayed well enough to win the French Derby. Desert Style is responsible for Paco Boy (Queen Anne Stakes) and for Bachir (Irish and French 2000 Guineas).

DANEHILL

Danehill, like Green Desert, was placed in the 2000 Guineas; like him he showed his best form over sprint distances (the Haydock Sprint Cup was his principal success). Although his progeny were at their most effective from six furlongs to a mile, he succeeded in siring top-class winners at all distances and was a highly influential sire. Rock Of Gibraltar, who won the 2000 Guineas, Irish 2000 Guineas, St James's Palace Stakes and Sussex Stakes, was probably Danehill's most successful son over a mile. Rock Of Gibraltar sired the Eclipse Stakes winner Mount Nelson.

Other top-class performers over a mile to be sired by Danehill were the brilliant but enigmatic George Washington; the French 2000 Guineas winners Landseer, Clodovil (sire of the Falmouth Stakes winner Nahoodh) and Aussie Rules; and Banks Hill (Coronation Stakes and Breeders' Cup Filly & Mare Turf). Oratorio was successful in the Eclipse Stakes.

Sons and daughters of Danehill to record victories in top-class races in excess of a mile were the Derby winner North Light; the Irish Derby winner Desert King; Duke Of Marmalade (King George VI and Queen Elizabeth Stakes and Prince Of Wales's Stakes); Dylan Thomas (King George VI and Queen Elizabeth Stakes, Prix de l'Arc de Triomphe and Irish Champion Stakes), Peeping Fawn (Irish Oaks) and Westerner (Gold Cup).

Dansili was a son of Danehill who never quite managed to win a Group 1 race. But he is the sire of the Prix de l'Arc de Triomphe winner Rail Link and of the Grand Prix de Paris winner Zambezi Sun.

However, it is Danehill Dancer who has proved to date to be the most successful of Danehill's stallion sons. A high-class two-year-old and effective at up to seven furlongs, Danehill Dancer is the sire of Speciosa, (1000 Guineas), Mastercraftsman (Irish 2000 Guineas and St James's Palace Stakes), Again (Irish 1000 Guineas) and Where or When (Queen Elizabeth II Stakes).

The overwhelming superiority of the Northern Dancer line poses two questions. Firstly: will any other male line prove capable of mounting a challenge to that stirp? Secondly: which line is most likely to provide a suitable outcross for Northern Dancer blood?

NASRULLAH

Time alone will provide the answers to these questions. However there are other lines coming down from Nearco who can be considered to have a realistic chance of holding their own in top class international racing. Before the upsurge of the Northern Dancer line, Nasrullah had appeared to be the strongest of Nearco's sire sons. A brilliant but temperamental horse, Nasrullah was the winner of the Champion Stakes and ran third in the Derby. He stood in Ireland until 1951, in which year he headed the sires' list, being in second position in two subsequent seasons. He was exported to the United States of America, in which country he headed the sires' list five times. He was the sire of Never Say Die, the winner of the Derby and the St Leger (and the sire of the Derby winner Larkspur) and of Nearula, winner of the 2000 Guineas and the Champion Stakes. But the four horses through whom the male line of Nasrullah has seemed most likely to be perpetuated are Red God, Grey Sovereign, Bold Ruler and Never Bend.

RED GOD

Red God, who was bred in America, was a high-class two-year-old and stood in Ireland, where he headed the list of sires of two-year-olds. His outstanding son, both on the racecourse and at stud, was Blushing Groom, who was trained in France and was a brilliant horse at up to a mile, becoming the leading French two-year-old and winning the French 2000 Guineas at three years. Sold to the USA for $6 million by his owner, the Aga Khan, Blushing Groom, who died from kidney failure in 1992, took time to make his mark.

For a time the line of Blushing Groom appeared to be flourishing but it is not now as strong as it once was. Arazi, the champion two-year-old of his year both in Europe and the USA, has not come up to expectations as a sire. Nashwan, the only horse in the history of racing to win the 2000 Guineas, the Derby, the Eclipse Stakes and the King George VI and Queen Elizabeth Stakes in the same season, is now dead, but was responsible for two top-class colts in Swain, the winner of the Irish Champion Stakes and twice winner of the King George VI and Queen Elizabeth Stakes, and a Group 1 sire in the USA; and the Prix de l'Arc de Triomphe winner Bago, now at stud in Japan.

Blushing Groom's son Rainbow Quest, who was awarded the Prix de l'Arc de Triomphe on the disqualification of Sagace, was arguably the most successful British-based sire since the pattern race system began. But his sire line is not now so strong. His Derby-winning son, Quest For Fame, has enjoyed more success in the USA and Australia than in Europe. Spectrum, another son of Rainbow Quest, won the Irish 2000 Guineas and the Champion Stakes, and was the sire of Golan, whose successes included the 2000 Guineas and the King George VI and Queen Elizabeth

Stakes. But Spectrum was exported to South Africa and Golan is now standing as a jumping sire.

It is possible that Golan's full-brother, Tartan Bearer, who finished second in the Derby, may prove good enough to carry on the line. And Rainbow Quest's son Crowded House, a highly impressive winner of the Racing Post Trophy as a two-year-old, may prove that his victory was no fluke.

Rahy, a further son of Blushing Groom, sired two top performers in Fantastic Light and the Sussex Stakes winner Noverre. But the former was exported to Japan; the latter to India. Subsequently, Noverre's son Le Havre was successful in the French Derby.

Gladiatorus, a world-class performer, is a great grandson of Blushing Groom, through Sillenq and Silic.

NEVER BEND
Never Bend was the champion American two-year-old of his year and, like many sons of Nasrullah (including Red God) was impetuous, which may have accounted for his inability to win beyond nine furlongs. However, he sired two exceptional horses in Mill Reef and Riverman. Mill Reef, who was bred and owned by Mr Paul Mellon, was a very brilliant horse, being capable of top-class form in both the two-year-old races and also in the principal middle distance races at 3 and 4 years. His successes included the Derby, the Eclipse Stakes, the King George VI and Queen Elizabeth Stakes and the Prix de l'Arc de Triomphe. His owner generously consented to let him stand at the National Stud at Newmarket where he proved a most prolific sire.

His most successful sons were Reference Point, the winner of the Derby, St Leger and King George VI and Queen Elizabeth Stakes; Shirley Heights, the winner of the English and Irish Derbies; and Doyoun, the winner of the 2000 Guineas. Shirley Heights was the sire of another Derby winner in Slip Anchor – in his turn the sire of the smart filly User Friendly, who won the Oaks, Irish Oaks, St Leger and Grand Prix de Saint-Cloud. Shirley Heights's son Darshaan, the winner of the French Derby, was responsible for Mark Of Esteem, the winner of the 2000 Guineas and

Queen Elizabeth II Stakes. Shirley Heights was also the grandsire of the Derby winner High-Rise.

Mark Of Esteem became the sire of the Derby winner Sir Percy and of the 1000 Guineas winner Ameerat and demonstrated his versatility when begetting the top-class sprinter Reverence.

The stud career to date of Darshaan's son Dalakhani indicated a strong likelihood that he will carry on the Mill Reef line. The winner of nine races, including the Criterium International at two years, the French Derby and the Prix de l'Arc de Triomphe, Dalakhani is the sire with his first crop of Conduit, who won the St Leger, the Breeders' Cup Turf and the King George VI and Queen Elizabeth Stakes, and Moonstone, the winner of the Irish Oaks.

Mill Reef's son Doyoun was responsible for Kalanisi, who won the Champion Stakes and the Breeders Cup Turf; and also for Daylami, whose seven Grade/Group 1 victories included the French 2000 Guineas, the Eclipse Stakes and the King George VI and Queen Elizabeth Stakes. But Kalanisi became used as a jumping stallion and Daylami was exported to South Africa after having sired the Irish Derby winner Grey Swallow.

RIVERMAN

Riverman was the winner of the French 2000 Guineas. Although no match for Brigadier Gerard in the Champion Stakes, he was by far the more successful at stud. He was responsible for that excellent mare Triptych, the winner of 14 races, including the Irish 2000 Guineas, the Champion Stakes (twice) and the Coronation Cup (twice); Riverman was also the sire of the Prix de l'Arc de Triomphe winners Detroit and Gold River; and Irish River, who emulated his sire by winning the French 2000 Guineas.

Irish River is also the sire of Hatoof, the winner of the 1000 Guineas and the Champion Stakes. The survival of the line is most likely, however to come through Bahri, the winner of the St James's Palace Stakes and the Queen Elizabeth II Stakes; his son Sakhee, the winner of the Prix de l'Arc de Triomphe and Juddmonte International, and the last-named horse's son, the July Cup winner Sakhee's Secret.

GREY SOVEREIGN

Grey Sovereign was a very fast two-year-old, very closely related to the Derby winner Nimbus. But in spite of this connection he never managed to win over distances in excess of six furlongs and it was not anticipated that he would exert so strong an influence as a stallion. In recent years, however, his line has felt the effects of the growth of the Northern Dancer line.

The line has, however, a chance of survival through Verglas, a smart two-year-old and a winner of the Coventry Stakes, and his sons Silver Frost (the winner of the French 2000 Guineas) and Stormy River (a Group 1 winner in France). Verglas comes down from Grey Sovereign through Zeddaan and Kalamoun (both smart milers and winners of the French 2000 Guineas); through Kenmare; and through Highest Honor (both the last named two horses being milers of Group 1 standard).

Another extant Grey Sovereign line comes down from Grey Sovereign's son Fortino II, through the French 2000 Guineas winner Caro and the Breeders' Cup Mile winner Cozzene to Mizzen Mast, also a Grade 1 miler. In Europe a male line descendant of Caro secured the Prince Of Wales's Stakes at Ascot. This was Vision D'Etat, who had won the French Derby the previous year. Vision D'Etat descends from Caro via Kaldoun, Smadoun, a listed race winner, and the Grand Prix de Paris winner Chichicastenango.

BOLD RULER

Bold Ruler was the winner of 23 races in America, including the Preakness Stakes and was one of the most successful sires to stand at stud in America during the twentieth century. His son Secretariat was rated the greatest horse to have raced in America since Man O'War and won 16 races, including the American Triple Crown. Secretariat did not however exert a strong influence at stud and it was Bold Ruler's grandson Seattle Slew (also an American Triple Crown winner) who carried on the line in the USA through A.P Indy.

Bold Ruler's son Bold Lad (Irish-bred; there were two horses called Bold Lad), the champion two-year-old of his year, was the grandsire of the filly Kooyonga who won the Irish 1000 Guineas, Coronation Stakes and Eclipse Stakes. But this branch of the Bold Ruler line seems unlikely to survive in Europe.

ROYAL CHARGER

Royal Charger was the first stallion to be acquired by the newly formed Irish National Stud. Although he was a leading sire of winners in Europe, none of his European-bred sons succeeded in establishing a lasting line. He was exported to America in 1953 where his line continued through his son Turn-To, the champion two-year-old of America. Turn-To was the sire of Hail to Reason, the winner of the Preakness Stakes, and of Sir Gaylord.

Roberto, the most successful son of Hail To Reason in Europe, was the European champion two-year-old, the winner of the Derby and the Benson and Hedges Gold Cup (in which he beat Brigadier Gerard) at three years and the Coronation Cup at four years. He is the sire of the St Leger winner Touching Wood and the grandsire, through Red Ransom of the Oaks winner Casual Look and the Juddmonte International Stakes winner Electrocutionist; through Silver Hawk of the Derby winner Benny the Dip and the St Leger winner Mutafaweq; through Kris S of the Derby winner Kris Kin, the St James's Palace Stakes winner Dr Fong and the smart two year-old and promising sire Lucky Story; through Robellino of the 2000 Guineas winner Mister Baileys; and through Dynaformer of the St Leger winner Lucarno.

Another son of Hail To Reason to make his mark on European racing was Halo, the sire of the outstanding Sunday Silence, the winner in the USA of the Kentucky Derby and the Preakness Stakes. The last named horse has proved to be an outstanding success in Japan, but his principal claim to fame in Europe comes through his son Divine Light, the sire of the 1000 Guineas winner Natagora.

Sir Gaylord was responsible for Sir Ivor and Habitat. The former was "Horse of the Year" in 1968 and won the 2000 Guineas, Derby, Champion Stakes and Washington International.

Although he sired some top-class winners, (including Ivanjica, the winner of the French 1000 Guineas and the Prix de l'Arc de Triomphe)

Sir Ivor did not establish a surviving sire line in Europe, although it is strong in Australia through Zabeel and Octagonal. And although Habitat was champion miler of his year, a classic sire, and a leading sire of two-year-olds, he also failed to sire a successful stallion son.

DANTE

Dante, the most successful son of Nearco on the racecourse, was the winner of a wartime Derby. His most successful daughter was the Oaks winner Carrozza; his most successful son was Darius, the winner of the 2000 Guineas and the Eclipse Stakes. Darius, in his turn was the sire of the top-class miler Derring-Do, the winner of the Queen Elizabeth II Stakes.

Derring Do's son High Top, the winner of the Guineas, was a successful sire of winners. But his line has become more influential in the sphere of jumping.

Dominion, a top-class miler by Derring-Do, was the sire of Primo Dominie, a speedy two-year-old and a successful sire of winners. There are two sons of Primo Dominie representing the Dante male line in the sphere of Flat racing. These are the smart two-year-old Primo Valentino and Imperial Dancer, who belied his parentage by proving a top-class horse at a mile and a half.

FAIRWAY

Pharos's own-brother Fairway was equally successful as a sire and certainly superior as a racehorse, his twelve victories including the St Leger, the Eclipse Stakes and the Champion Stakes (twice).

Sadly the male line of Fairway now seems unlikely to survive. It is because the line produced so many outstanding horses that a brief summary has been included.

On the racecourse, Fairway's most successful son was Blue Peter, the winner of the 2000 Guineas, the Derby and the Eclipse Stakes. Blue Peter was the sire of Ocean Swell (Derby and Ascot Gold Cup) and Botticelli (Ascot Gold Cup and Italian Triple Crown), but he failed to establish an extant line.

The disappearance (almost certainly through theft) of Shergar, before had had a chance to prove himself at stud, and the premature death of Troy between them contributed largely to the near demise of the Fairway line. Shergar, who won the Derby, the Irish Derby and the King George VI and Queen Elizabeth Stakes, came down from Fairway through the Champion Stakes winner Honeyway and the top-class miler Great Nephew. The latter horse was also the sire of Grundy, who won the Derby, the Irish 2000 Guineas, the Irish Derby and the King George VI and Queen Elizabeth Stakes. Grundy was exported to Japan but not before he had sired the Oaks winner Bireme.

In spite of his early demise, Troy (successful in the Derby, Irish Derby and King George VI and Queen Elizabeth Stakes) succeeded in siring two top-class fillies in Helen Street and Walensee. He descended from Fairway through Fair Trial, through the Eclipse Stakes winner Petition and through the top-class miler Petingo.

Petition, the grandsire of Troy, was responsible for the very brilliant filly Petite Etoile. Possessed of a lightning turn of foot, Petite Etoile won the 1000 Guineas, the Oaks, the Yorkshire Oaks, Champion Stakes and Coronation Cup (twice).

Petition's son March Past, a high-class performer over the shorter distances, sired the Lockinge Stakes winner Queen's Hussar. The latter sired Highclere, who won the 1000 Guineas and the French Oaks in the colours of the Queen, and the exceptional Brigadier Gerard. The winner of seventeen of his eighteen races, he won the 2000 Guineas, Eclipse Stakes, the Champion Stakes (twice), the Sussex Stakes (twice) and the King George VI and Queen Elizabeth Stakes. Although responsible for the St Leger winner Light Cavalry and for the disqualified Champion Stakes winner Vayrann, Brigadier Gerard was a comparative failure as a sire.

SICKLE AND PHARAMOND

Of the own-brothers Sickle and Pharamond II, the line coming down from the latter is stronger in the USA than in Europe. Sickle, who ran third in the 2000 Guineas, has exerted a strong influence both in the

USA, to which country he was exported, and in Europe. In America he sired Unbreakable, the winner of the Victoria Cup whose son Polynesian was the sire of Native Dancer. This outstanding horse won 22 of his 23 races, including the Preakness Stakes and the Belmont Stakes, his sole defeat coming in the Kentucky Derby in which he finished second. Native Dancer became known as the "Gray ghost of Sagamore" denoting the stud on which he was reared. The most influential of his sons were Raise A Native, the champion American two-year-old, Dan Cupid and Atan.

DAN CUPID

Dan Cupid became the sire of Sea-Bird, the greatest of all male line descendants of Phalaris and one of the greatest horses to race on the turf. His seven victories from eight starts included the Derby (which he won by five lengths) and the Prix de l'Arc de Triomphe, again by five lengths, in spite of swerving when entering the straight. Bred in France by his owner, Monsieur Jean Ternyck, Sea-Bird was syndicated for the then formidable figure of $1,350,000 to stand in America. His outstanding winner was the mare Allez France, who won the French 1000 Guineas, French Oaks, Prix de l'Arc de Triomphe and Prix Ganay. Through his son Arctic Tern, Sea-Bird became the grandsire of the French Derby winner Bering. The latter went on to sire the 2000 Guineas winner Pennekamp and the French 2000 Guineas winner American Post.

ATAN

Atan, who stood in Ireland, was the sire of Sharpen Up, the winner of the Middle Park Stakes and a very successful sire in England prior to his exportation in 1980 to the USA. His most successful daughter was Pebbles, who won the 1000 Guineas, Eclipse Stakes and Champion Stakes. He also sired the own-brothers Kris and Diesis, both prolific sires of winners. Kris was a top-class miler and sired two sons who answered to that description in Sure Blade and Flash Of Steel. Neither of these two succeeded at stud, but Kris was responsible for two top-class mares in Oh So Sharp (1000 Guineas, Oaks and St Leger) and a further Oaks winner in Unite.

Diesis, the winner of the Dewhurst Stakes, stood in America throughout his stud career but enjoyed great success in Europe. His daughters Diminuendo and Ramruma both achieved the Oaks, Yorkshire Oaks and Irish Oaks treble, whilst Love Divine provided her sire with a further Oaks win. The most successful of the sons of Diesis is Halling, the only horse in racing history to have achieved the Eclipse Stakes-Juddmonte International double in successive years. Halling has proved to be a successful in-depth stallion.

Although he was never a fashionable sire, Diesis's son Elmaamul, also a winner of the Eclipse Stakes, sired a top-class colt in Muhtathir, the sire in his turn of two Group 1 winners in Satwa Queen and Doctor Dino.

Selkirk was a son of Sharpen Up who proved to be top-class at a mile, his victories including the Queen Elizabeth II Stakes. He has proved a most successful sire, his 11 Group 1 winners including Wince, the winner of the 1000 Guineas. There is still a chance that Selkirk may sire a colt who is good enough to carry on the line. A further son of Sharpen Up to make the top-grade is the Prix de l'Arc de Triomphe winner Trempolino, who is the sire of the Queen Anne Stakes winner Valixir.

RAISE A NATIVE

Raise A Native was the sire of Alydar, who won the Florida Derby and proved a most successful stallion in America. Exclusive Native, a son of Raise A Native, was the sire of Affirmed, the winner of the American Triple Crown and later syndicated for the then record sum of $17,000,000.

MR PROSPECTOR

The most influential member of the Native Dancer male line in Europe is, however, Mr Prospector, the champion older sprinter in America and a winner at up to seven furlongs. The line from Mr Prospector has flourished to such an extent that it may conceivably pose a threat to the supremacy of the Northern Dancer line. The most successful of Mr Prospector's progeny to race in Europe are Ravinella (1000 Guineas and French 1000 Guineas), Kingmambo (French 2000 Guineas and St James's Palace Stakes), Distant View (Sussex Stakes) and the top-class two-year-old Machiavellian.

GONE WEST

Zafonic, a miler of exceptional ability, was sired by the good Mr Prospector horse Gone West. The St James's Palace Stakes winner Zafeen and the top-class two-year-old Xaar were Zafonic's most successful sons. Zamindar, a full-brother to Zafonic, has proved to be a most successful sire of fillies. The most notable of these is the Aga Khan's Zarkava, the winner of the French 1000 Guineas, French Oaks and Prix de l'Arc de Triomphe. Darjina and Zenda were also winners of the French 1000 Guineas.

Elusive Quality and Mr Greeley are other sons of Gone West to influence European racing. Elusive Quality is the sire of the very smart miler Raven's Pass, who won both the Queen Elizabeth II Stakes and the Breeders Cup Mile. Mr Greeley is the sire of Finsceal Beo, the winner of the English and Irish 1000 Guineas, and of Reel Buddy, who won the Sussex Stakes.

GULCH

The Mr Prospector horse Gulch is responsible for Harayir, the winner of the 1000 Guineas, and for Nayef. The last-named, a half-brother to Nashwan, is the winner of four Group 1 races, including the Champion Stakes and the Juddmonte International, and is already the sire of a Group 1 winner in Tamayuz.

WOODMAN

The Mr Prospector horse Woodman is the sire of Bosra Sham, successful in the 1000 Guineas and Champion Stakes; for the Eclipse Stakes winner Hawk Wing; for Hector Protector, the winner of the French 2000 Guineas and for Hula Angel, the winner of the Irish 1000 Guineas.

SEEKING THE GOLD

The above horse is the sire of the world class performer Dubai Millennium, whose money earnings of over £2½ million included the Prince Of Wales's Stakes, Dubai World Cup and St James's Palace Stakes. Dubai Millennium died tragically after only one season at stud, but succeeded in becoming the sire of the Irish 2000 Guineas winner Dubawi.

DISTANT VIEW

The Sussex Stakes winner was responsible for Observatory, the champion three-year-old miler in Europe, the winner of the Queen Elizabeth II Stakes and the sire in his turn of the Group 1-winning filly African Rose.

MISWAKI

This speedy son of Mr Prospector sired the Prix de l'Arc de Triomphe winner Urban Sea (later the dam of the Derby winners Galileo and Sea The Stars) and the Irish 2000 Guineas winner Bachelor Duke.

MACHIAVELLIAN

This very high-class two-year-old was to have his highly successful stud career cut short by his premature death. Storming Home, the winner of the Champion Stakes, Street Cry and Almutawakel, both winners of the Dubai World Cup, Medicean, who won both the Eclipse Stakes and the Lockinge Stakes and the Coronation Stakes winner Rebecca Sharp were his best progeny. Street Cry is the sire of the Group 1 winner Majestic Roi; Medicean sired the Coronation Stakes winner Nannina.

KINGMAMBO

The French 2000 Guineas winner is the progenitor of that excellent colt Henrythenavigator, described by his trainer, Aidan O'Brien, as "the best horse I have ever trained." Henrythenavigator won eleven races, including the English and Irish 2000 Guineas, the St James's Palace Stakes and the Sussex Stakes. King's Best, a further son of Kingmambo, won the 2000 Guineas and went on to sire the Sussex Stakes winner Proclamation and Creachadoir, successful in the Lockinge Stakes. Rule Of Law proved a superior stayer to his sire when winning the St Leger.

The most successful of Kingmambo's daughters in Europe were Divine Proportions (French 1000 Guineas and French Oaks), Russian Rhythm (1000 Guineas, Coronation Stakes and Lockinge Stakes) and Virginia Waters (1000 Guineas).

It is vital for the future of thoroughbred breeding that enough sire lines emerge to prevent the male line of Northern Dancer from obtaining too exclusive a monopoly. The unthinking dictum that "it is impossible to have too much of a good thing" is unlikely, if carried to extremes, to prove to be of benefit to the industry.

CHAPTER 5:

THE PEDIGREE – THE FEMALE LINE

When the term "family" is used in relation to the thoroughbred horse it is not intended to refer to his sisters or his cousins or his aunts. The only correct usage of the term is in connection with the direct line of female descent in that animal.

There are three reasons why thoroughbred families are classified in this manner. The first is that the system of recording mares in the General Stud Book (see chapter 7) makes it easier to classify families by this means than by any other. The second is that whilst there are only three surviving male lines there are fifty female lines still in existence. Since the surviving lines of female descent are more numerous than those of male descent they provide a better basis for differentiating between the family groups.

The third reason why thoroughbred families are classified by line of female descent is based upon the fact that whilst a top-class stallion may serve upwards of 100 mares in a season a mare is mated only once a year. It therefore follows that a stallion may sire a thousand foals in the same time that it takes, a mare, even if she is the best of breeders, to produce ten foals. And even then her chances of producing live foals can be reduced by barrenness, slipping foal (miscarrying) or stillbirth. Above all she may produce only a small percentage of fillies amongst her live foals. It follows that while the male line descendants of a successful sire can run, within five generations, to tens of thousands, the number of mares or fillies descending in direct female line from a famous broodmare will be strictly limited in number.

From a purely hereditary point of view the value of "family" must be limited. No foundation mare, however strong her influence, can make more than a small contribution to the hereditary make-up of her more remote descendants. Perhaps the most significant point in relation to families is that many breeders strongly believe in their importance. The late Leon Rasmussen, who was for nearly forty years the principal bloodstock correspondent of *Daily Racing Form*, America's main daily racing publication, wrote "I am a family man, preferring family over individuals." In other words, Rasmussen held so strong a belief in the value of good families that he preferred to buy a mare belonging to one of these families, but with a defect in conformation, than a good individual from a lesser family. Many breeders feel that if they cannot afford to buy a top-class racemare for stud, then family is the next most important thing.

The strong belief in the value of families may have some value in practical terms. Mares from highly esteemed families tend to be mated with top-class stallions and the line receives an infusion of genes that are liable sooner or later to result in the breeding of a successful racehorse. Also as a result of being more propitiously mated, mares from the more fashionable families stand a better chance of breeding top-class racehorses than do those mares from lesser families.

There is no doubt that the strong belief in the value of families endows them with a commercial value. Membership of a fashionable family helps all the mares, fillies, foals and yearlings which belong to it. Although most breeders prefer mares or fillies who have won a race of some description, they have been known to lay out considerable sums on non-winning mares or fillies who belonged to the "right" families.

One set of circumstances that sets the female line apart from the male line is the contact between each foal and its dam. At no stage of his career does a stallion have any contact with his progeny. A mare however has a long period of contact with her foal both during the pre-natal period and in the four months prior to weaning. During this period the foal will become subject to strong influences from the mare. It must be remembered that the mare, when a foal, was in her turn subject to just such influences from her dam, who was subject to the same influences from her dam, etc., etc. In this manner the distaff element of the pedigree can play a stronger part in shaping the career of each foal than can the male element – even though it is an influence of environment rather than of heredity.

Up until the middle of the Nineteenth Century there was widespread belief that the stallion and thus the sire line were the elements in the pedigree that mattered. The first person to focus attention upon the female element in the pedigree was Bruce Lowe, whose contribution to bloodstock breeding will be discussed in detail in the next chapter. An individual who believed very strongly in the omnipotence of the distaff element in the pedigree was the German Friedrich Becker, who was the author of *The Breed of The Racehorse*. Sire lines, he argued, could not keep going under their own power. They came and went, but the female lines kept going for ever. Becker's statement was correct but the reasoning behind it was wrong. The contrast between the number of surviving male and female lines can be explained by the fact that a mare can only have one foal a year whilst a stallion can sire 100 or more. In consequence mares can be drawn from a wide field, whilst all but the best stallions can be eliminated. Any person who owns a thoroughbred mare will always think in terms of breeding from her. The result being that an unpromising mare (i.e. a mare with a poor pedigree and racing record) has the chance not only to prove a success at stud but also, in some instance, to found a strong female line. The very moderate and unfashionably bred mare Maid of Kilcreene was to become the fourth dam of Mumtaz Mahal and Lady Juror, the founders of two of the most successful of modern families. Female lines survive for the above reasons and not because they possess superior qualities to the male lines.

One other argument of Becker's requires attention. He stated that during its pre-natal union with the mare the foal was subject to influences which counteracted the genes of the sire. Again he was wide of the mark. As has been explained the contact between mare and foal is unquestionably important. But a foal's hereditary make-up is decided unchangeably at the formation of the first body cell. Modern science therefore demonstrates that Becker's views are untenable.

Although the great majority of the most important winners in the history of racing are descended in direct female line from the fifty "foundation" mares in the first volume of the *General Stud Book*, these mares, unlike the three foundation sires cannot claim a monopoly of the winners of these races. This is because the Rules of Racing have never precluded Non Thoroughbred horses from racing against thoroughbreds and, in consequence, a number of the most important races have been won by horses belonging to "obscure" families. The word obscure implies that there is no means of establishing a tail-female link between the first known mare in these families and any of the mares in the original volume of the *GSB*. Some of these are American families, whose foundation mares were exported to the USA before the publication of the *GSB*. But in many cases families became obscure through breeders in the past having failed to maintain proper records. The subject of Non Thoroughbreds will be dealt with in the chapter on the *General Stud Book*.

In 1957 the late Captain Kazimierz Bobinski published his *Family Tables Of Racehorses*. This was the first work to record the direct female line descent of all the major winners in racing history both at home and abroad. In this work, Bobinski incorporated all the families in the *GSB* "classified" by Bruce Lowe, adhering to their family numbers. The remaining families were classified by designating the first known mare in each family as the foundation mare. Non thoroughbred families of American origin were classified as A1, A2, A3 etc; such families as were of British or Irish origin he classified as B1, B2, B3 etc.

Although the numbers assigned to each family by Bruce Lowe constitute a convenient form of classification they are seldom used in modern times. Families are more often named after individual mares, mostly foaled within the last fifty or sixty years, who had earlier founded vigorous branches of old lines or given them fresh impetus.

The 1994 classic races illustrate the comparative irrelevance of referring to families by their numbers. Mister Baileys, Las Meninas, Erhaab and Moonax, the winners respectively of the 2000 Guineas, 1000 Guineas, Derby and St Leger all belonged to number 1 Family. It is true that the immediate female family of Erhaab possessed a visible connection with that of Moonax. Moonstone, the latter's fifth dam, was the seventh dam of the Derby winner. Apart from that, however, the common ancestress in the tail-female line is too remote to be of any great significance.

It would require a separate book to trace in detail all the female families. However, some of the more important families (in particular those who are prominent in modern times) will be considered.

ALOE NO 2 FAMILY
(Foundation Mare; THE BURTON BARB MARE)
This is a very prominent branch of No. 2 Family. Aloe was an own-sister to the Ascot Gold Cup winner Foxlaw and her dam was a half-sister to the dam of the Derby winner Call Boy. Aloe has exerted her influence through her daughters Feola, Sweet Aloe and Aroma. Feola was bred at the Sandringham Stud and raced in the Royal colours. She finished second in the 1000 Guineas and third in the Oaks. She was the dam of Hypericum (1000 Guineas), Angelola (Yorkshire Oaks) and Above Board (Yorkshire Oaks and Cesarewitch). She was the grandam of Aureole (winner of the King George VI and Queen Elizabeth Stakes and a leading sire) Round Table (Horse of the Year in America and a successful sire), Sideral (many times champion sire in Argentina) and Above Suspicion (St. James's Palace Stakes). Feola is also the third dam of Highclere (1000 Guineas and French Oaks); the fourth dam of Height of Fashion (Princess of Wales's Stakes); and the fifth dam of Nashwan (2000 Guineas, Derby, Eclipse Stakes and King George VI and Queen Elizabeth Stakes), Pebbles (1000 Guineas, Eclipse Stakes and Champion Stakes) and Unfuwain (Princess of Wales's Stakes and successful sire). Nayef (Champion Stakes) and Ghanaati (1000 Guineas) also belong to the family.

Sweet Aloe was the grandam of Alcide (St. Leger and King George VI and Queen Elizabeth Stakes), the third dam of Parthia (Derby and Jockey Club Cup) and sixth dam of Salsabil (1000 Guineas, Oaks, Irish Derby and Prix Vermeille) and Marju (St. James's Palace Stakes). Aroma was the fourth dam of Known Fact (2000 Guineas) and fifth dam of Gone West (sire of the 2000 Guineas winner Zafonic).

DALMARY NO 5 FAMILY
(Foundation Mare; OLD EBONY)

This mare, who won the Yorkshire Oaks, produced two successful daughters in Rough Shod II and Jennydang. Jennydang was the grandam of Tudor Era, who won the Washington International but was later disqualified, the third dam of Lorenzaccio (Champion Stakes and the sire of Ahonoora) and the fourth dam of Thatching (July Cup and a successful sire). By far the more influential of the daughters of Dalmary was Rough Shod II, who, though exported to America, has exerted a strong influence on both sides of the Atlantic. She was the dam of Ridan (Florida Derby), Gambetta (Debutante Stakes) and Mocassin (champion two-year-old of her year). She is the grandam of Thatch (champion two-year-old, leading miler at three years and a successful sire), Lisadell (Coronation Stakes), Gamely (Group 1 Beldame Stakes, twice) and Apalachee (a leading two-year-old in Europe, won Observer Gold Cup). Rough Shod II was also the third dam of Drumtop (Canadian International Championship) and Nureyev (champion miler in France and a successful sire). Only four generations removed from Rough Shod II were Sadler's Wells (Irish 2000 Guineas, Eclipse Stakes and 14 times champion sire), Fairy King (successful sire) and Topsider (successful sire in America).

LADY JOSEPHINE NO. 9 FAMILY
(Foundation Mare; THE VINTNER MARE)

Lady Josephine, a very fast mare in her own right, was the dam of the "Flying filly" Mumtaz Mahal and of Lady Juror, winner of the Jockey Club Stakes. Lady Juror was the dam of Fair Trial (a leading sire), the grandam of Tudor Minstrel (2000 Guineas and a leading sire) Commotion (Oaks) and Neolight (Coronation Stakes); the fourth dam of Kashmir II (2000 Guineas) and the seventh dam of Sayyedati (1000 Guineas). Mumtaz Mahal was the dam of Mirza II (Gimcrack Stakes), the grandam of Mahmoud (Derby in record time), Nasrullah (Champion Stakes and five times leading sire in the USA), Rivaz (Queen Mary Stakes) and Abernant (champion sprinter and successful sire).

She was the third dam of Migoli (Eclipse Stakes and Prix de l'Arc de Triomphe), Royal Charger (Sussex Stakes and a leading sire in Europe and USA) and Prince Taj (a leading sire in France). She was also the fourth dam of Petite Etoile (1000 Guineas, Oaks, Champion Stakes and Coronation Cup, twice) and Ginetta (French 1000 Guineas). In addition Mumtaz Mahal was the fifth dam of Oh So Sharp (1000 Guineas, Oaks and St Leger) and Kalamoun (French 2000 Guineas and a successful sire); the sixth dam of On The House (1000 Guineas and Sussex Stakes); and the seventh dam of Shergar (Derby, Irish Derby and King George VI and Queen Elizabeth Stakes) and Shantou (St. Leger). Recent members of the family include Alborada (Champion Stakes, twice), Ameerat (1000 Guineas) Alamshar (Irish Derby and King George VI and Queen Elizabeth Stakes) and Aussie Rules (French 2000 Guineas).

PRETTY POLLY NO. 14 FAMILY
(Foundation Mare; OLDFIELD MARE)

This brilliant racemare, who won the 1000 Guineas, Oaks and St Leger, was ancestress through her four daughters Polly Flinders, Molly Desmond, Dutch Mary and Baby Polly of such notable performers as Brigadier Gerard (2000 Guineas, Eclipse Stakes, King George VI and Queen Elizabeth Stakes and Champion Stakes, twice); St Paddy (Derby, St Leger and Eclipse Stakes), Flying Water (1000 Guineas and Champion Stakes), Psidium (Derby), Premonition (St. Leger), Only For Life (2000 Guineas), Shadayid (1000 Guineas), Carroll House (Prix de l'Arc de Triomphe), Supreme Court (King George VI and Queen Elizabeth Stakes), Great Nephew (sire of Grundy and Shergar), Nearctic (sire of Northern Dancer), Luthier (Champion sire in France), Don II (French 2000 Guineas) and Donatello II (Italian Grand Prix and sire of Crepello). Marling (Irish 1000 Guineas, Coronation Stakes, Sussex Stakes), Russian Rhythm (1000 Guineas and Coronation Stakes), Love Divine (Oaks), Swain (King George VI and Queen Elizabeth Stakes, twice), Cape Cross (successful sire) and Brian Boru (St Leger) are members of the family to have made a mark in the past two decades.

SCEPTRE NO. 16 FAMILY
(Foundation Mare; SISTER TO STRIPLING)

Sceptre, the only horse in history to win four English classics (the 2000 Guineas, 1000 Guineas, Oaks and St Leger) founded a strong line through her daughters Maid of the Mist, Coronation IV, Queen Empress, Queen Carbine and Curia. Sceptre was the grandam of Craig An Eran (2000 Guineas and Eclipse Stakes) and Sunny Jane (Oaks) and ancestress of Buchan (Eclipse Stakes, twice), Saltash (Eclipse Stakes), Tiberius (Ascot Gold Cup), Full Dress II (1000 Guineas), Commanche Run (St. Leger), One in a Million (1000 Guineas), Petition (Eclipse Stakes and sire of Petite Etoile), Zucchero (Coronation Cup), Taboun (2000 Guineas), Match III (King George VI and Queen Elizabeth Stakes), Relko (Derby, French 2000 Guineas and Coronation Cup) and Reliance II (French Derby).

CHAPTER 6:

BRUCE LOWE

A very wide gulf exists between the findings of the modern scientist and the theories expounded by Bruce Lowe. Nevertheless the researches Lowe carried out more than a hundred years ago have continued to benefit thoroughbred breeding. He greatly increased our store of knowledge of the thoroughbred; and he established a very convenient method of classifying thoroughbred families.

At this juncture, therefore, it is necessary to give a brief account of his work. Lowe, an Australian by birth, undertook the task, during the nineteenth century, of tracing every mare who was in the General Stud Book at that time, back to its original root. A German named Herman Goos set about the same task, and, although both men worked independently, the conclusions at which they arrived were generally similar. Both of them found that every horse traced back to one of fifty mares in the original volume of the *G.S.B.* (It has since been maintained that the number of foundation mares in the *G.S.B.* is no more than 27 – but no findings on the subject have yet been finalised).

Bruce Lowe allotted the figure 1 to the family which, at the time of his researches, numbered amongst its descendants the most winners of the Derby, Oaks and St Leger; the remaining families were allocated numbers in order of how many winners of these races they possessed to their credit. But when he came to Family No. 43, Lowe found that no classic winner belonged to it. He therefore numbered this and all the remaining families according to his opinion of their merit.

Although it is no longer true to say that these families remain classified in order of their important winners there is one invaluable contribution that Bruce Lowe has made to modern thoroughbred breeding. The lowest numbered families have maintained to the present day a far higher overall level of productivity than those with the high numbers. Even if they have produced more "also rans" they continue through sheer weight of numbers to produce a higher level of winners.

It must not be taken that every individual mare from No. 1 Family is, for example, a more productive breeder than a mare from No. 43 Family. But the overall level of production in the low-number families is in general far in excess of those with high numbers.

Lowe found that families 1 to 5 were particularly strong in top-class racehorses; he therefore designated these Running Families. He also found that families 3-8-11-12-14 were strong in the stallion element. These he termed Sire Families. He claimed that there was no classic winner not carrying a strain in the first three removes of either a "running" or "sire" family.

This latter claim can still be upheld over a hundred years later, and in consequence his insistence that members of high-number families were unlikely to do well, unless inbred to low-number families or mated to partners with "running" or "sire" blood. Lowe did not maintain that good results came only from "running" or "sire" families; but he advocated that members of high-number families should be crossed with this blood.

Having explained the strengths of Bruce Lowe it is necessary also to examine his weaknesses. Lowe believed that superior qualities were the property of "running" and "sire" families in perpetuity. He believed in other words that such qualities were anchored in the female chain of descent, i.e. passed down from mother to daughter. Modern genetics has shown that qualities are not the sole property of bloodlines, whether male or female, and that genetic (hereditary) characteristics can be transmitted through numerous different routes. And a horse's hereditary make-up is dependent primarily not on bloodlines but on genotype, in other words the combination of genes which he receives from his parents.

It is impossible to support Lowe's belief in the superiority of "Running" or "Sire" families. In the first instance, many of the outstanding racehorses of the twentieth and twenty-first centuries are not members of running families. Nijinsky and The Minstrel belong to No 8 family. Shergar, Tudor Minstrel, Galileo, Sea The Stars and Henrythenavigator to No 9 family, Rock of Gibraltar to No 10 family, Ouija Board to No 12 family, Brigadier Gerard to No 14 family, New Approach to No 19 family, and Mill Reef to No 22 family.

In the second instance many of the most successful twentieth and twenty-first century stallions belong to families not classified as "sire" families. Notable amongst these were Northern Dancer and Danehill who belong to No 2 family, Ribot (No 4 family), Sadler's Wells (No 5 family) and Mr Prospector (No 13 family).

The American bloodstock market is another factor which has devalued the results of Lowe's researches. The value of the dollar has caused many breeders to orientate their policy to what the American breeders require – and speed is to the latter more important than stamina. Since few races in America are run over distances in excess of a mile and a half American breeders have little interest in the progeny of essentially staying stock. Leading breeders have in consequence concentrated on the production of fast stock and the result has been that the longer-distance races have declined in prestige.

The Derby remains the "Blue Riband" of the Turf. The St Leger, however, since it is run over a mile and three quarters, persistently fails to attract the leading three-year-olds of each generation and is no longer held in its former high esteem.

As has been mentioned earlier Bruce Lowe rated the families in order of the number of victories in the Derby, Oaks and St Leger which each foundation mare could claim amongst her descendants. He deliberately omitted the 2000 Guineas and the 1000 Guineas from his calculations, since he considered these races unimportant. Modern trends have resulted in the 2000 Guineas now being held in higher esteem than the St Leger, and the fact that Lowe did not take the first-named race into account can certainly give rise to the argument that the most important of modern families are not necessarily those designated by him in numerical order.

Yet the low-numbered families still continue to produce large amounts of high-class horses and Captain Bobinski certainly had his task of compiling his *Family Tables of Racehorses* greatly facilitated by Bruce Lowe's researches. The value of Lowe's work must be considered indispensable taken in its modern context as an integral part of the Bobinski tables.

CHAPTER 7:

THE GENERAL STUD BOOK (GSB)

The General Stud Book is the official genealogical record of the thoroughbred breeding industries of both Great Britain and Ireland. The work is owned, compiled, printed and published by Weatherbys, who reserve the right to decide what horses can be admitted to, excluded or removed from its pages.

No horse is allowed to run under the Rules of racing unless it has been registered either in the *GSB* or in the *Register of Non Thoroughbred Horses*, which will be enlarged upon later in this chapter. All foals must be registered within four months of their birth and all registrations must be accompanied by a Foal Identification Certificate (issued by a qualified veterinary surgeon), a Certificate of Covering (issued by the stallion owner) and a Breeding Certificate (issued by the mare owner).

The parentage of all foals is determined through a DNA test after a blood sample has been obtained from each foal. All thoroughbred foals are micro-chipped.

To be admitted to the *General Stud Book* a horse must be able either:

(1) To be traced down all lines of its pedigree to horses registered before 1st January 1980 in
(a) *The General Stud Book*, and /or
(b) Any of the following Stud Books;
   The American Stud Book, the French Stud Book, the Stud Books of Argentina, Australia, Austria, Barbados, Belgium and

Luxembourg, Brazil, Chile, Colombia, Cyprus, Czech Republic, Denmark, Dominican Republic, Ecuador, Emirates, Germany, Greece, Guatemala, Hungary, India, Israel, Italy, Japan, Kenya, Malaysia, Mexico, Morocco, Netherlands, New Zealand, Norway, Panama, Paraguay, Peru, Philippines, Poland, Portugal, Slovak Republic, South Africa, Spain, Sweden (A-Register), Switzerland, Trinidad and Tobago, Uruguay and Venezuela.

OR

(2) To prove satisfactorily eight recorded crosses consecutively with horses qualified as in category 1 above, including the cross of which it is the progeny and to have satisfied the performance and approval conditions as set out below.

For the purposes of the *General Stud Book*, horses in categories 1 and 2 above are designated "Thoroughbred."

CONDITIONS AS IN CATEGORY 2.

The foal can show in both the "Thoroughbred" and "Non-Thoroughbred" sections of its pedigree, such performances in races open to "Thoroughbreds" as to warrant its assimilation with "Thoroughbreds."

The promotion is approved by the unanimous agreement of the *International Stud Book* Committee.

James Weatherby published *An Introduction to the General Stud Book* in 1791 and the first volume of the *GSB* made its appearance seventeen years later. The word 'General' was used to differentiate it from the many private stud books which were kept by breeders of that period. Weatherby's purpose in publishing the book was to correct the 'increasing evil of false and inaccurate pedigrees.' However, he did not define the qualifications for entry to the *GSB*. Although he implied the existence of the term 'thoroughbred' by using the word 'half-bred' in relation to animals who could not be admitted, he did not clarify what was meant by 'thoroughbred'. In consequence, problems were to arise over the terms on which horses could be admitted to the *GSB*.

There were two factors which made these problems more acute. The first was that Non Thoroughbred horses (a term more accurate than the loosely used 'half-bred') had always been allowed to race against thoroughbreds. The second was that foreign-bred horses had always been accepted in the *GSB* if they were in the Stud Books of their country of origin; and in certain cases, notably the United States of America, the pedigrees of some of these horses were not without flaw. This was because the stud book authorities of many foreign countries admitted horses on terms less stringent than those laid down for entry to the *GSB*.

The American breeding industry began to expand and Weatherbys were forced to take a closer look at the possible consequences. They took the unprecedented step of asking the advice of the Stewards of the Jockey Club; and the outcome of their deliberations was the first qualifying test for admission to the *GSB*. The qualification was that 'any animal claiming admission should be able to prove satisfactorily eight or nine crosses of pure blood to trace back for at least a century and to show such performances of its immediate family on the Turf as to warrant belief in the purity of the blood.'

Although a considerable number of American horses raced in England during the nineteenth century, the vast majority were returned to America when the time came for them to go to stud. As long as this state of affairs continued the amended qualification served its purpose as a safeguard. But it was to prove inadequate in the face of the events which were to take place in America.

During the first decade of the twentieth century a series of anti-gambling laws were passed in the United States which were to bring racing in America virtually to a standstill for a number of years. The result was that the racing authorities in England had visions of animals of doubtful pedigree being imported by the shipload. The horse, who was to be at the centre of the controversy was Lexington. This horse, who had been the leading sire in America on no less than eighteen occasions, exerted an influence comparable to that of St Simon in England, and appeared in the pedigrees of most American racehorses. Although he traced back to

Diomed in direct male line, Lexington was out of a mare with very suspect elements in his pedigree. The breeding fraternity understandably felt that if so influential a horse as Lexington possessed a doubtful pedigree, how much more suspect must be the pedigrees of the many greatly inferior horses now likely to be imported to England. The very understandable concern felt both by the authorities and by breeders led to a tightening-up of the conditions under which horses could be admitted to the GSB.

This culminated in what is now termed the 'Jersey Act'. As the result of a meeting in 1913, the editors of the *General Stud Book*, acting on the advice of Lord Jersey, the then Senior Steward of the Jockey Club, inserted a new rule for qualification. "No horse or mare can, after this date, be considered as eligible for admission unless it can be traced without flaw on both sire's and dam's side of its pedigree to horses and mares themselves already accepted in the earlier volumes of the Book."

The act was to cause considerable friction between the British and the Americans. The latter saw it as an attempt to exclude them from the world bloodstock markets; the English maintained that they were only trying to keep the blood pure.

The Act was not retrospective. It permitted horses already in the Book to remain whilst excluding new horses who were similarly bred. Had the Act been retrospective, many of the strongest influences in modern bloodstock would have been excluded from the GSB. Nearco, the grandsire of Northern Dancer, would have been ineligible for the GSB on the grounds that his third dam, Sibola, was American-bred. And Mumtaz Mahal and Lady Juror, the half-sisters who founded powerful female dynasties, would have been excluded through the American nationality of Americus, the sire of their second dam, Americus Girl.

An even more harmful result of the Act, however, was that many of the most successful strains of blood and many winners of the most important races became excluded from the GSB. An outstanding example was Tourbillon, four times champion sire in France and possibly the outstanding stallion in the history of French breeding. His maternal grandsire Durbar II (incidentally a winner of the Derby) was termed 'half-bred' through being out of an American mare; Banshee, the grandam of Tourbillon, possessed a high ratio of American blood in her pedigree. Eventually the proliferation of successes by 'half-breds' in the major European races became an embarrassment to the English racing authorities and in 1949 it was decided to repeal the Act. The new qualification now read 'Any animal claiming admission from now on must be able to prove satisfactorily some eight or nine crosses of thoroughbred blood, to trace back for at least a century and to show such performances on the Turf as to warrant belief in the purity of the blood.' The clause 'to trace back for at least a century' was later deleted; it is the number of generations that is today considered important – and not the time-span.

The amended terms for entry to the *GSB* regularised the position of Tourbillon and his descendants within its pages, also the position of the majority of American-bred horses. But much harm had been done in that, by boycotting Tourbillon and his sons on account of their 'half-bred' status, breeders cut themselves off from a useful source of progress. During the 36 years of the "closed shop" the emergence of several new generations had resulted in the "impure" strains becoming too remote to possess any great significance; the clause covering eight or nine crosses now covered most of the disputed strains. But a similar enactment made in 1913 would not have served the required purpose, since many American horses could not then claim eight or nine crosses of thoroughbred blood.

The motives which prompted the Jersey Act were undoubtedly, on the whole, well-intentioned, to ensure that the animals within the *GSB* bred true – in other words were genetically similar. It is easy, with the benefit of hindsight, to condemn the breeders of the pre World War I generation for the attitudes which led to the passing of the Jersey Act; and it is important to understand how the situation must have appeared to them at the time.

The new regulations which governed entry to the *GSB* were more than adequate to deal with disputed strains of American origin. But there still remained the problem of Non Thoroughbred horses of English and Irish origin. Before 1972, Weatherbys would accept registrations for racing purposes from horses who were not in the *GSB*. But they did not maintain any authentic family records of horses who answered this description. The only publication which recorded non-thoroughbred family records was the *Half-Bred Stud Book*, which was compiled by Miss Frances Prior. In 1972 it was realised that the non-thoroughbred horses, who by that time represented 12% of all horses registered, constituted a problem which required attention. The Jockey Club, who were consulted, decided to regularise the position by forming the Register of Non Thoroughbred Horses, thus in effect taking over the work previously done by Miss Prior.

It was discovered that many members of non-thoroughbred families had become eligible for the *General Stud Book* by virtue of their own racing performances (and/or those of their close relations) and the fact that they had now acquired eight or more crosses of thoroughbred blood. One such family was that of the very speedy Hycinthia Girl, who became the dam of Gay Mairi, the winner of the Nunthorpe Stakes (one of the most prestigious of the sprint races), the dam in her turn of Montgomery, the champion sprinter in France.

One of the families in the 'Half-Bred Book' was promoted to *GSB* status, in spite of the fact that none of its members had acquired sufficient thoroughbred crosses to meet the criteria laid down by the Stud Book authorities. This family is known as the 'Verdict' Family. The foundation mare Verdict was a high-class and courageous mare, who won both the Coronation Cup and the Cambridgeshire; but neither her sire Shogun (once a fancied Derby candidate) or her dam Finale were thoroughbred. Verdict was therefore doubly 'half-bred'. She bred the very high-class and courageous mare Quashed, winner of the Oaks and Ascot Gold Cup; Thankerton, who ran third in the 2000 Guineas and Derby; and Dictum, who won the Ebor Handicap. All three of these horses were by thoroughbred sires and therefore each possessed one cross of thoroughbred blood. Lavant, a great granddaughter of Verdict bred two top-class sprinters in Lucasland and So Blessed, the latter (who achieved a measure of success as a sire) having been considered a likely contender for the 2000 Guineas.

In view of the family's achievements, Messrs Weatherby took the step, which they could only do in exceptional circumstances, of exercising their right as proprietors and publishers and admitting the family to the *GSB*. The Irish 1000 Guineas winner Sonic Lady, and Petorius, a pattern race winner at two and three years and later a fairly successful sire, did much to vindicate Messrs Weatherbys' decision.

It was, however, the mare Attraction who provided the Verdict family with its most recent claim to fame. The only filly to achieve the treble of the 1000 Guineas, Irish 1000 Guineas and Coronation Stakes, she also added the Sun Chariot Stakes to the list of her Group 1 victories.

In order that greater liaison should be brought about between the Stud Book authorities of different countries in discussions on breeding records, transfer of horses between stud books, artificial insemination etc, it was decided in 1976 to set up the International Stud Book Committee. The main achievements of the Committee to date are as follows:

(1) Uniform policies towards parentage testing (see the beginning of this chapter)
(2) Unanimous agreement on identification techniques
(3) The prohibition of artificial breeding (i.e. artificial insemination or the transfers of embryos)
(4) That horses should be "promoted" to Stud Books only by international agreement
(5) The need to establish the Status of World Stud Books.

CHAPTER 8:
INBREEDING

To those who do not understand the implications, the word "inbreeding" is synonymous with degeneracy. The term conjures up visions of an animal who is a poor specimen, lacking in substance, unsound and of uncertain temperament. But many breeds of farm and domestic animals have been created by intensive inbreeding; the method was, for example, followed by the Colling Brothers when they were developing the breed of Shorthorn cattle. And a very high percentage of the most important winners in the history of racing have been the outcome of planned inbreeding.

The most simple definition of inbreeding is "the mating of closely related individuals." All thoroughbreds are in-bred in relation with most human societies; a modern racehorse has, in a single generation not very far back, an aggregate of ancestors which outnumbers the entire foundation stock of the breed. This can only have come about as a result of inbreeding. In the case of the thoroughbred inbreeding implies a closer relationship between the two animals mated than the average of the breed; the normal implication is that the ancestor common to both parents is duplicated within the first four generations of the offspring of the mating.

The purpose of inbreeding is to reproduce the genes of an ancestor in double strength; in other words to increase the influence of that ancestor. Inbreeding serves to diminish the influence of other ancestors and in consequence the single offspring of an inbred mating is likely to resemble the duplicated ancestor more closely than it would do if the same ancestor appeared only once in its pedigree. The influence of the duplicated ancestor – whether for better or for worse – is thus extended over an increased number of generations.

In his excellent publication *The Classic Pedigree* (published in 1989), Michael Church, projects manager for the *Racing Post*, tabulated the pedigrees of the winners of the five English classic races, the King George VI and Queen Elizabeth Stakes and the Prix de l'Arc de Triomphe from 1776–1989. His researches revealed that no fewer than 504 individual winners of these races possessed a duplicated ancestor within the first four generations of their pedigrees; and that although, in the majority of cases, the duplicated ancestor appeared twice in the fourth generation, very many of the horses mentioned were more closely inbred.

Since 1989 more of the above races have been won by horses who are the outcome of planned inbreeding. Authorized (*see over*), the winner of the Epsom Derby in 2007, and a very highly-rated winner of that classic, is inbred in the third and fourth generations to Northern Dancer (in other words inbred 3x4, or inbred at one free generation). Northern Dancer is his great grandsire in direct male line, and is also the great-grandsire of his dam Funsie.

It will be noticed that, in the majority of cases, the duplicated ancestor will be a stallion whose racing ability combined with his influence as a progenitor makes him a suitable vehicle through which to carry out inbreeding plans.

A further example of inbreeding to Northern Dancer is provided by the outstanding miler Rock Of Gibraltar (*see over*). He is inbred 3x3 to the great stallion – in other words Northern Dancer appears twice in his pedigree in the third generation. Northern Dancer is the grandsire of Danehill, himself the grandsire of Rock Of Gibraltar, and is also the grandsire of the latter's dam Offshore Boom.

However there have been numerous instances throughout the history of breeding in which the duplicated ancestor is a mare. An influential broodmare can also be an adequate vehicle through which to inbreed, irrespective of her own racing record. If she can claim top-class winners amongst her descendants it is considered that she possesses the right genes.

Henrythenavigator (*see over*), to whom I have referred in Chapter four is an example of inbreeding to a mare, being inbred 4x4 to the outstanding

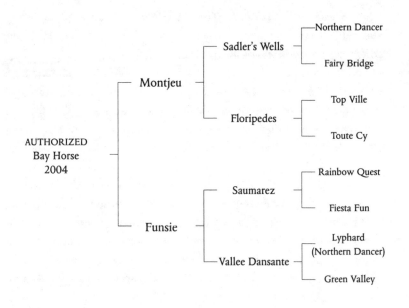

AUTHORIZED
Bay Horse
2004

- Montjeu
  - Sadler's Wells
    - Northern Dancer
    - Fairy Bridge
  - Floripedes
    - Top Ville
    - Toute Cy
- Funsie
  - Saumarez
    - Rainbow Quest
    - Fiesta Fun
  - Vallee Dansante
    - Lyphard (Northern Dancer)
    - Green Valley

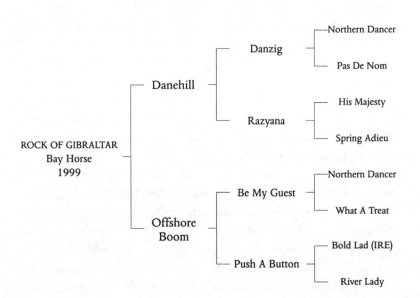

ROCK OF GIBRALTAR
Bay Horse
1999

- Danehill
  - Danzig
    - Northern Dancer
    - Pas De Nom
  - Razyana
    - His Majesty
    - Spring Adieu
- Offshore Boom
  - Be My Guest
    - Northern Dancer
    - What A Treat
  - Push A Button
    - Bold Lad (IRE)
    - River Lady

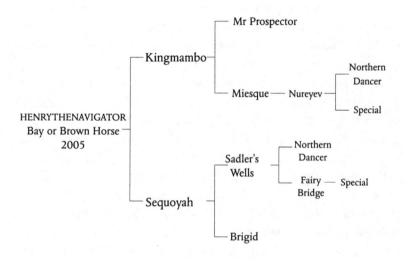

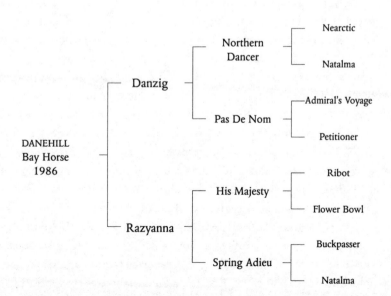

mare Special. The latter mare appears both as the dam of Nureyev, the maternal grandsire of Kingmambo, the sire of Henrythenavigator; and as the dam of Fairy Bridge, whose son Sadler's Wells is Henrythenavigator's maternal grandsire. Special comes into Henrythenavigator's pedigree through separate sources.

Danehill, a very fast sprinter and also one of the most influential sires of the present day, is a striking example of inbreeding to a mare, being inbred 3x3 to Natalma. The last named mare is the dam of Danehill's grandsire Northern Dancer and she is also Danehill's great grandam in direct female line.

The steady growth of the thoroughbred population which has taken place over the past two hundred years has meant that there have been progressively more stallions than there were in the late eighteenth century (when the shortage of suitable stallions necessitated close inbreeding). In consequence there has been relatively little inbreeding closer than 3x4. There were, however, two notable exceptions in the years following the second war.

The mare Coronation V may seem a somewhat "dated" example, since she was in training during the 1940s. She has been included because she represents an exceptional case of very close inbreeding. Coronation V was a very brilliant racemare who was bred and owned by the late Monsieur Marcel Boussac. As a two-year-old she won the Queen Mary Stakes over five furlongs at the Royal Ascot meeting and the Prix Robert Papin. At three years she dead-heated with her stable companion Galgala in the French 1000 Guineas and she ran out a brilliant winner of the Prix de l'Arc de Triomphe. Thus she showed top-class ability over distances ranging from five furlongs to a mile and a half; she was defeated in both the English and Irish Oaks, but she can be forgiven these reverses since she was clearly feeling the effects of travelling.

Being a daughter of Djebel (by Tourbillon) and Esmeralda (by Tourbillon), Coronation V was thus inbred to Tourbillon in the second generation or was inbred 2x2 to that stallion; she has also been described as being inbred to Tourbillon at "no free generations." (She was also, incidentally,

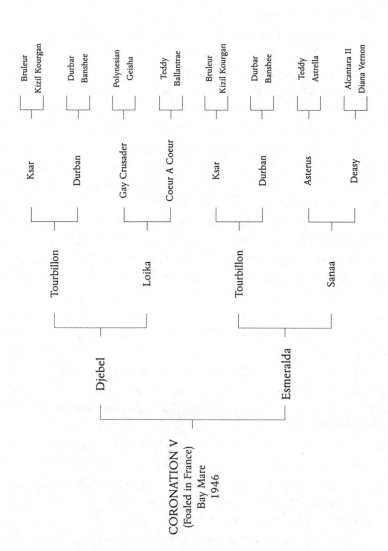

CORONATION V
(Foaled in France)
Bay Mare
1946

Djebel

Tourbillon
Ksar
Bruleur
Kizil Kourgan
Durban
Durbar
Banshee

Loika
Gay Crusader
Polynesian
Geisha
Coeur A Coeur
Teddy
Ballantrae

Esmeralda

Tourbillon
Ksar
Bruleur
Kizil Kourgan
Durban
Durbar
Banshee

Sanaa
Asterus
Teddy
Astrella
Deasy
Alcantara II
Diana Vernon

inbred 4x4 to the influential French stallion Teddy). Coronation failed to conceive during her fourteen years at stud and many people cited her close inbreeding as the cause of her infertility. But since her full sister bred perfectly normally at stud, this does not seem likely.

Another top-class racehorse closely inbred to Tourbillon was Hugh Lupus, who was the winner of the Irish 2000 Guineas and the Champion Stakes. At stud Hugh Lupus became the sire of Hethersett, who won the St Leger and was the progenitor in his turn of the Derby winner Blakeney. Hugh Lupus was by Djebel (by Tourbillon) out of Sakountala (by Goya II, by Tourbillon). He was, in bloodstock breeding terminology, inbred 2x3, or at "one free generation" to Tourbillon.

E. Fitch Daglish, writing in the *British Racehorse*, stated "whether the results of inbreeding are satisfactory or the reverse, will depend entirely on the material subject to its influence and the care with which it is applied." It is important that any vehicle for inbreeding whether horse or mare should be prepotent for desirable characteristics. Peter Willett, in his *Introduction to the Thoroughbred*, describes a prepotent thoroughbred as one who possesses a reasonable number of genes in double strength. For our purpose that last description is probably the most apt. Prominent amongst the twentieth century stallions who proved themselves to be possessed of prepotent qualities are Hyperion, Nearco (the grandsire of Northern Dancer), Nearco's son Nasrullah, Man O'War and Tourbillon.

The instances quoted above denote inbred matings that have succeeded. It is important however to be aware of the risks involved. Some of the genes (units of inheritance) which are carried as recessive (dominated genes which may reappear in future generations) may control such characteristics as unsoundness, nervous trouble, infertility, roaring etc.

For this reason the person who inbreeds is taking considerable risks. Clearly no stallions or mares who are unsound are suitable breeding material. But the problem may go deeper. Sound animals may carry harmful recessives which could be brought to the surface in double strength. An unsound sire is bound to pass on this unsoundness to some of his progeny if this is a flaw in his hereditary make-up. Some of his progeny who do

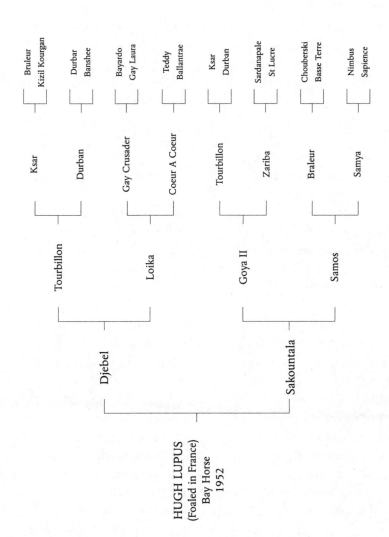

HUGH LUPUS
(Foaled in France)
Bay Horse
1952

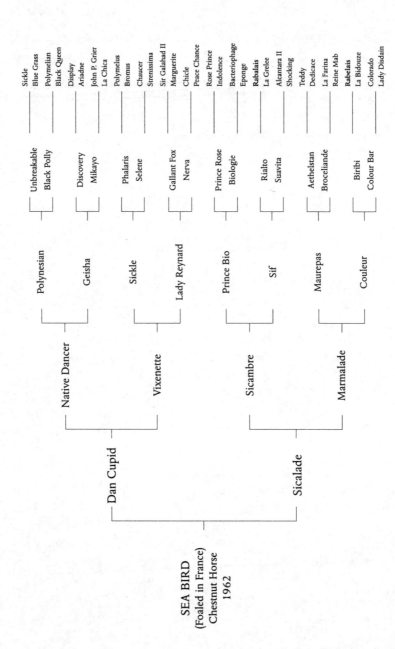

SEA BIRD
(Foaled in France)
Chestnut Horse
1962

Dan Cupid

Native Dancer

Polynesian
- Unbreakable
  - Sickle
  - Blue Grass
- Black Polly
  - Polymelian
  - Black Queen

Geisha
- Discovery
  - Display
  - Ariadne
- Mikayo
  - John P. Grier
  - La Chica

Vixenette

Sickle
- Phalaris
  - Polymelus
  - Bromus
- Selene
  - Chaucer
  - Serenissima

Lady Reynard
- Gallant Fox
  - Sir Galahad II
  - Marguerite
- Nerva
  - Chicle
  - Peace Chance

Sicalade

Sicambre

Prince Bio
- Prince Rose
  - Rose Prince
  - Indolence
- Biologie
  - Bacteriophage
  - Eponge

Sif
- Rialto
  - **Rabelais**
  - La Grelee
- Suavita
  - Alcantara II
  - Shocking

Marmalade

Maurepas
- Aethelstan
  - Teddy
  - Dedicace
- Broceliande
  - La Farina
  - Reine Mab

Couleur
- Biribi
  - **Rabelais**
  - La Bidouze
- Colour Bar
  - Colorado
  - Lady Disdain

not show this characteristic may carry it as a recessive, which may be disclosed by inbreeding. It is up to breeders to weigh up the risks against the possible advantages.

Line breeding is a less intensive form of inbreeding and the difference between the two is undefined. It has been suggested that line breeding implies a matching between a stallion and a mare both of whom belong to the same family. Thatching, a high-class sprinter and a classic sire (although his line has since gone under), was an example of the above. The common ancestress in this case is the mare Dalmary, who is the third dam in tail-female line both of Thatch, the sire of Thatching, and also the fourth dam in tail-female line of Abella, who is Thatching's dam.

The term line breeding has, however been used to denote a horse, one of whose male ancestors traces to the same mare as his dam. Danehill (see above) may be considered a horse of this type. Natalma is the dam of his grandsire Northern Dancer as well as being his great grandam in direct female line.

Line breeding is less effective than inbreeding in that the hereditary characteristics of the selected ancestor are not so well preserved. Outside genes are introduced at each generation and for this reason the approach to the possession of important genes in double strength is slower. On the other hand the chances of uncovering harmful recessives are reduced.

Heterosis, or hybrid vigour is the phenomenon of increased vigour which sometimes occurs when genetically different animals are mated. With thoroughbred horses heterosis is most likely to be found when individuals representing two separate inbred lines are mated. The two lines may be complementary the one holding characters which the other lacks and vice versa. This is what seems to have happened in the case of Sea-Bird, whose racing career is recounted in Chapter 4. Sea-Bird possessed no duplicated ancestor within the first four generations of his pedigree. But his sire Dan Cupid is inbred 4x2 to Sickle. The latter horse is not only the great grandsire of Dan Cupid in tail-male line; he is also that horse's maternal grandsire. Sicalade, the dam of Sea-Bird, is inbred 4x4 to Rabelais, who is mentioned in Chapter 4 as the direct male ancestor of

Ribot. Rabelais did not appear in the pedigree of Dan Cupid; Sickle did not appear in the pedigree of Sicalade.

Dan Cupid, although he was third in the French Derby, did not succeed in winning over that distance. Sicalade raced only once, later being sold for butcher's meat. However she was a daughter of the top-class middle-distance performer Sicambre, the winner of the French Derby and Grand Prix de Paris, and so possessed many genes which made for stamina — offsetting the relative lack of this attribute in Sea-Bird's sire.

Once a successful inbreeding has succeeded in bringing about the necessary important characteristics in double strength it is advisable to mate the resultant offspring with an unrelated animal. "Breed in to fix type; breed out to secure vigour," has long been a maxim with thoroughbred breeders.

CHAPTER 9:

THE PEDIGREE AS A GUIDE TO STALLION SELECTION

The late Atty Persse, who trained The Tetrarch, was once asked what he considered the most important qualities in a racehorse. He replied "speed – more speed – still more speed."

Persse was correct in asserting the priority of speed. Races are not won by staying in the same place. But speed, like all other qualities, is relative. The ultimate test of a fast horse is whether he can defeat the best of his contemporaries over the minimum distances of five or six furlongs. Sir Charles Leicester considered that a degree of speed was a sine qua non for a successful stallion. In his authoritative work *Bloodstock Breeding* he wrote "a horse must have top speed to transmit to his stock."

The trainer of The Tetrarch was, however, wrong to emphasise the single aspect of speed to the exclusion of soundness, courage and consistency. A breeder should exercise extreme caution in sending a sprint-bred mare to a sprinting stallion. It is true that a mating of this type has certain practical advantages; some Group 1 races are now run over five and six furlongs. From a purely commercial point of view the odds are in favour of a speed orientated mating. David Dinkis wrote in the *Thoroughbred Record* "Speed sells. Stamina does not." There are however limits to the use of a purely sprint-bred horse on a racecourse, since the majority of the most valuable races are contested between a mile and a mile and a half and he is unlikely to be effective over such distances. (Although there have been sprint-bred horses who were effective beyond sprint distances – notably Millkom who won the Group 1 Grand Prix de Paris over ten furlongs.)

Because a horse showed all his best form at the minimum distance, it does not follow that his best stock will have the same stamina limitations; Grey Sovereign, Red God, Sharpen Up, Ahonoora and recently Danehill and Pivitol are examples of sprinters who became influential stallions. But it is unlikely that this would have come about without the aid of mares who were either effective at distances of a mile or over or were bred to be effective over these distances.

While it is a mistake to overestimate the influence of speed it is an even greater mistake to overestimate the importance of stamina. There is always a danger that the mating of two horses who showed their best form at a mile and a half or more (regardless of how good these two horses may be) may result in an excess of stamina at the expense of speed.

The middle distance stallions (that is those whose best performances were recorded at a mile and a half or more) are of limited value to all breeders except those in the very highest income brackets. Unless a horse can win the very most important races over this distance (i.e. the Derby, the Irish Derby, the King George VI and Queen Elizabeth Stakes and the Prix de l'Arc de Triomphe) he will not be considered a good commercial proposition. A horse who does succeed in winning one of these races is likely to acquire a stud value which will make him too expensive for all but a minority of breeders.

Stallions who were effective over distances between five furlongs and a mile and a quarter on the racecourse can prove a worthwhile proposition for the majority of breeders even if they cannot afford to use the best material. Speed, consistency, soundness and a high fertility are likely to be found in horses in the above categories, quite apart from their commercial viability. Inability to stay a mile and half need not be a bar to success at stud. Northern Dancer's sole defeat came about in the mile and a half of the Belmont Stakes, whilst Sadler's Wells was more effective at ten furlongs than at twelve.

The most expensive stallions are not always the best. Queen's Hussar commanded a fee of £250 at the time he covered the dam of Brigadier Gerard. Ahonoora began his stud career at a fee of £2500. Red God, the grandsire of Nashwan and Rainbow Quest, stood in Ireland at a fee of 98 guineas, a very low figure even by the standards of the pre-inflationary 1960s.

The commercial viability of a prospective stallion is an indispensable factor which must be taken into account when a mating is planned. The breeder who uses a fashionable sire will greatly increase his chances of producing a yearling that will sell well – and this will prove a great "safety net." But it is a great mistake to plan a mating solely with the sale ring in mind. If the stallion and mare are not compatible in terms of conformation and temperament; if the mating will involve inbreeding to an ancestor who is not prepotent for the right reasons; if the mating is likely to produce an animal who is too small or too big: the likelihood of the produce developing into a good racehorse must be very remote indeed.

Racecourse performance must be the most important criteria by which a stallion should be judged: if he was a good racehorse he is liable to possess the right genes, although it will take time to discover whether he is capable of transmitting these to his progeny. It is also advisable to choose a stallion whose sire was a good progenitor of stallions; but if a prospective stallion is not the son of a good sire of sires, then it is important to look for a famous name on the dam's side of the pedigree.

It cannot be emphasised too strongly that breeding is an inexact science. The best planned of matings using the best stallion and broodmare material cannot be guaranteed to produce a good racehorse. Nevertheless a breeder can increase his chances of success by planning his matings methodically. For example many families produce better results when mated to horses of a certain stallion line than they do with other lines. The descendants of the mare Black Ray have enjoyed conspicuous success when mated to horses of the Nasrullah male line – the results being such as Blushing Groom, Mill Reef and Wollow, winner of the 2000 Guineas and Eclipse Stakes. A breeder can discover the sires of the important winners in his mare's family and select a suitable horse from one of those sire lines.

There are many instances in which two lines of blood achieve far better results when mated together than when mated elsewhere. When this happens a "blood nick" is said to occur. For example, horses of the Nasrullah male line achieved excellent results with those of the male line of Round Table. Nasrullah was fiery and impetuous; Round Table was phlegmatic. One line of blood, therefore, complemented the other.

It is important for a breeder when he is planning a mating to see what the pedigree of the resultant foal will look like. For this reason many breeders use what are known as "split pedigree" books. These are loose-leaf books in which the tabulated pedigree of the mare can be set against those of prospective mates and the bloodlines and inbreeding patterns of the future produce (assuming that the mare produces a live foal) can be examined.

There are many people who are sceptical on the subject of the conventional breeding methods and maintain that only the science of genetics can provide the true answer. At the present time, however, our knowledge of the subject is too limited for matings to be planned on a purely genetic basis; and until that time comes, it is preferable to use methods that have achieved a measure of success, even though they may have their limitations.

CHAPTER 10:

A WELL BALANCED PEDIGREE

Although a number of sprint races have been accorded Group 1 status, the majority of the most important and valuable races on the turf are contested over distances ranging from a mile to a mile and a half. It can therefore be suggested that the ideal pedigree is that which contains the correct balance of speed and stamina.

On balance speed must be considered the most important single factor. The horse who lacks a turn of foot will have little chance of competing with the best of his contemporaries in the most valuable races. However a mating between two sprinters is unlikely to produce a horse who is effective over a mile in top-class company. In the opinion of many breeders, the miler is the ideal stallion. But again the mating of a miler to a miler is not likely to result in a top-grade ten-furlong performer, let alone a horse who is effective over a mile and a half in the same grade. I have mentioned earlier that the person who mates a twelve-furlong mare to a twelve furlong sire runs the risk of over developing stamina at the expense of speed.

No breeder, however, should make the mistake of regarding stamina as a redundant factor. The vast majority of winners of the Derby (and of the other major mile and a half events) possessed either a sire, a dam or a maternal grandsire who were effective over a mile and a half. However it is preferable that a twelve-furlong mare should be mated with a stallion whose maximum distance was ten furlongs and the reverse is also true. There have been instances in which horses with "ten-furlong" pedigrees have shown top-class ability at a mile and a half. Erhaab, the winner of the 1994 Derby, is a good example. His sire, Chief's Crown, never won beyond ten furlongs; his dam, Histoire, was never successful over distances in excess of ten and a half furlongs; and the maximum winning distance of his maternal grandsire, Riverman, was nine furlongs. A "ten furlongs plus" pedigree, such as that of Erhaab, can entitle a horse to win the Derby.

As a normal rule a breeder will not obtain a winner of a top-grade race over a mile and a half by mating a miler with a ten-furlong horse. But a notable exception occurred in the case of Ouija Board, whose wins included the Oaks, the Irish Oaks, and two runnings of the Breeders' Cup Filly & Mare Turf. Ouija Board was sired by the miler Cape Cross. Selection Board, the dam of Ouija Board, raced only twice, finishing second as a two-year-old, so it was hard to discover her ideal distance. But she was a full-sister to Teleprompter, who had won the valuable Arlington Million over ten furlongs. It seemed, therefore, that Ouija Board would not be troubled to stay a mile and a quarter but that a mile and a half might pose problems for her. Happily this proved not to be the case.

The ability of the top-class sprinter Danehill to sire top-class middle-distance horses has been referred to earlier in the volume. But it is interesting to consider the cases of two of his sons both of whom succeeded in winning the King George VI and Queen Elizabeth Stakes – Dylan Thomas and Duke of Marmalade.

Dylan Thomas subsequently won the Prix de l'Arc de Triomphe and there is no doubt that he was a genuine middle-distance performer. But his grandsire Diesis did not win beyond seven furlongs and can hardly have been an influence for stamina. It is possible that Lagrion, the dam of Dylan Thomas may have injected some staying genes into her son. Although she did not win, she was capable of staying a mile and a half and her dam was a half-sister to a winner of the Lingfield Oaks Trial.

The situation in the case of Duke Of Marmalade was different. His dam, Love Me True, never won beyond a mile and the same applied to her sire, Kingmambo. The sole success of Lassie's Lady, the grandam of Duke Of Marmalade, came in an event over seven furlongs. It is therefore hard to know how Duke Of Marmalade was able to win a top-class race over a mile and a half. Lassie Dear, the third dam of Duke Of Marmalade, was a half-sister to Gay Mecene, a top grade middle-distance performer; but the staying element in the pedigree appears too remote to have exerted any noteworthy influence.

When he contested the Ascot race, Duke Of Marmalade was undoubtedly helped by the firm underfoot conditions which prevailed on the day and this factor enabled him to make the best use of his speed. But his subsequent defeat in the Prix de l'Arc de Triomphe indicates that he did not truly stay a mile and a half.

Breeding is not an exact science and from time to time horses not apparently bred to stay will belie their pedigrees by doing so, and staying bred horses may be capable of producing unexpected speed. But if a horse's stamina appears suspect, it is better to be cautious about his ability to stay until he proves that he can do so.

A horse whose pedigree represented an adequate balance of speed and stamina was Nashwan (*see over*). This horse did not possess the speed or the precocity to win one of the valuable early-season two-year-old races. In this respect his achievements fell short of those of other top-class middle-distance horses such as Fairway, Hyperion and Bahram in the years between the wars and Brigadier Gerard and Mill Reef in more recent times.

Nashwan won both the races which he contested as a two-year-old. But both races were contested late in the season over seven furlongs and a mile; and neither were events of pattern status. It was at three years that Nashwan revealed his true ability. He became the only horse in history to win the 2000 Guineas, the Derby, the Eclipse Stakes and the King George VI and Queen Elizabeth Stakes in the same season. Thus he proved himself superior to the best of his contemporaries at a mile, at ten furlongs, and at a mile and a half – a feat seldom achieved by the present day thoroughbred.

Sheikh Hamdan Al Maktoum, the breeder of Nashwan, had had access to the very best breeding material. Blushing Groom, Nashwan's sire, was

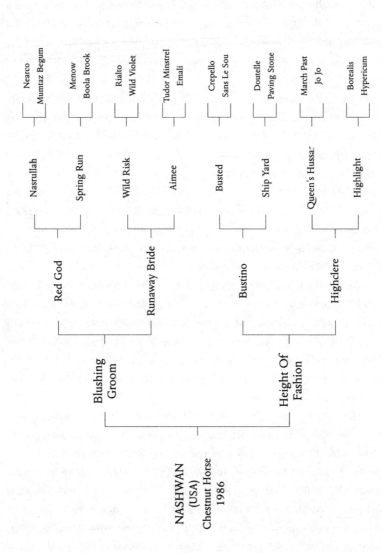

NASHWAN
(USA)
Chestnut Horse
1986

Blushing
Groom

Red God

Nasrullah

Nearco
Mumtaz Begum

Spring Run

Menow
Boola Brook

Runaway Bride

Wild Risk

Rialto
Wild Violet

Aimee

Tudor Minstrel
Emali

Height Of
Fashion

Bustino

Busted

Crepello
Sans Le Sou

Ship Yard

Doutelle
Paving Stone

Highclere

Queen's Hussar

March Past
Jo Jo

Highlight

Borealis
Hypericum

a really high-class horse who had the speed to defeat the highest class opposition at sprint distances (he won the Group 1 Prix Robert Papin over five and a half furlongs as a two-year-old) and the stamina to beat the best of his contemporaries over a mile. His successes at the latter distance included the Grand Criterium at two years and the French 2000 Guineas at three years. Blushing Groom never proved himself over long distances. His one attempt at a mile and a half was in the Derby, in which he failed to stay and finished third. Syndicated to stand at the Gainesway Stud in Kentucky, he proved a most successful stallion; but the majority of his best progeny (with the notable exception of Rainbow Quest, Snow Bride and Jalmood) were not effective over distances in excess of a mile and a quarter.

In the case of Blushing Groom stamina limitations cast a shadow over an otherwise brilliant career. But there was no lack of this attribute in Height of Fashion, the dam of Nashwan. This mare, who was bred and raced by the Queen, was sold privately to Sheikh Hamdan for a figure reportedly in the region of £1,000,000. She won two races over a mile and a half as three-year-old including the important Princess of Wales's Stakes. But her defeats in the Yorkshire Oaks and the King George VI and Queen Elizabeth Stakes indicated that she just lacked that turn of speed that is so vital in a winner of a Group 1 race. As a two-year-old, however, she had won all three of her starts including two pattern races – the May Hill Stakes and the Fillies' Mile. Bustino, the sire of Height of Fashion, although a late developing horse, possessed plenty of staying ability, being the winner of the St Leger and the Coronation Cup (in record time) and having finished second in a very close finish with Grundy for the King George VI and Queen Elizabeth Stakes. Height of Fashion's dam, Highclere, won the 1000 Guineas and the French Oaks (at ten furlongs); she was a daughter of the miler Queen's Hussar out of Highlight, who won twice over a mile and half and was by the Coronation Cup winner Borealis out of Hypericum, also winner of the 1000 Guineas.

Nashwan's pedigree represented an excellent combination of speed and stamina. Red God, the sire of Blushing Groom, was a headstrong horse, like so many sons of Nasrullah. Bustino was an ideal vehicle through which to offset this impetuousness, being somewhat "laid back" like his sire Busted and his grandsire Crepello. In many ways Blushing Groom and Bustino complemented each other. Blushing Groom supplied the speed, brilliance and precocity lacking in the maternal grandsire; Bustino provided the stamina, durability and equable temperament.

Twenty years were to elapse before Sea The Stars was to follow in Nashwan's footsteps and win both the 2000 Guineas and the Derby. Sea The Stars, like Nashwan, was sired by a top-class miler out of a mare with abundant stamina. Cape Cross never won beyond a mile, the distance of the Lockinge Stakes (the most important win of his career) and was a son of the sprinter Green Desert. Sea The Stars went on to win the Eclipse Stakes, Juddmonte International and the Prix de l'Arc de Triomphe.

Although Urban Sea, the dam of Sea The Stars, was sired by Miswaki (whose maximum winning distance was a mile) there is no doubt that she was a top-class performer at a mile and a half, her eight wins in France including the Prix de l'Arc de Triomphe. She had also bred a Derby winner in Galileo. As in the case of Nashwan, the sire provided the speed; the dam the stamina.

It is because speed is the prime quality in a racehorse that a number of sprinters have exerted an influence at stud. Red God and Grey Sovereign are earlier examples. A more recent example is Ahonoora, who surprised many students of breeding by becoming the sire of the Derby winner Dr Devious. However, unlike most of those sprinters whose influence became widespread, Ahonoora did not possess a purely sprinting pedigree. His sire, Lorenzaccio, was the winner of the Champion Stakes and his maternal grandsire was Martial, the winner of the 2000 Guineas.

Other sprinters who have exerted a strong influence on the breed are Ahonoora's son Indian Ridge, Sharpen Up, Danehill, Green Desert and Pivotal.

The horse who is bred purely for speed has an important part to play in the breeding of the thoroughbred. An example of such a horse is to be found in Bahamian Bounty, who is located at the National Stud at Newmarket. Bahamian Bounty was sired by Cadeaux Genereux, all of whose best performances were recorded over sprint distances (although he did win a pattern race over seven furlongs). Clarentia, the dam of Bahamian Bounty, was a fast two-year-old, but did not win beyond sprint distances. Ballad Rock, the maternal grandsire of Cadeaux Genereux, likewise never won in excess of six furlongs.

It seemed unlikely that Bahamian Bounty would stay the mile of the French 2000 Guineas, for which he started – and so it proved. At stud he is the sire of the top-class sprinters Pastoral Pursuits and Goodricke – the first of this duo having made a promising start at stud.

Speed is the single factor that is common both to the sprinter and the Derby winner and without this attribute the racing and stud prospects of any horse will be strictly limited. But this quality will serve a wider range of purposes if allied to stamina.

CHAPTER 11:

THE BREEDING OF JUMPERS

Senator Federico Tesio, the breeder of Nearco and Ribot, maintained that the ability to jump was not hereditary. He wrote in *Breeding The Racehorse*: "The function creates the organ and in fact jumpers do develop a certain set of muscles, but this required character is not passed on to the offspring." Because a horse is successful as a sire on the Flat it does not follow that he will become a successful sire of jumpers. It is also a fact that none of the best progeny of a Flat-race sire are put to jumping. In many cases, horses sire winners both on the Flat and over jumps; but as a rule top-class sires of Flat racers and jumpers divide into different categories.

This can be explained by the fact that Flat racers and jumpers are called upon to perform different tasks. The Flat-race horse races mostly in spring and summer, never has more than ten stone on its back and in an ordinary season runs on good or firm going. The jumper races throughout the winter, has to carry 12 stone and possess the courage to jump; and, in the majority of cases, has a line of purely jumping blood close up in its pedigree. (It is, however, important to qualify the last statement by pointing out that horses with high-class Flat-race pedigrees have a better record in hurdle races, the emphasis on speed being greater in races of this category than in steeplechases. Persian War, See You Then and Istabraq – all of whom were triple Champion Hurdle winners – possessed Flat-racing pedigrees of the highest class. Istabraq, in fact, was very closely related to the Epsom Derby winner Secreto).

One of the difficulties of breeding jumpers is that, owing to the fact that a chaser seldom reaches its best before the age of six, it takes a long time to discover whether the progeny of a sire are going to be good jumpers; and in some cases the sire is past his prime, or even dead, by the time that he has made his name. Two examples of such sires are Crash Course and Oats, both of whom had died by the time the breeding public had become aware of their ability. Crash Course sired the Grand National winner Rough Quest and the Cheltenham Gold Cup winner Jodami amongst numerous other top-class jumping performers. Oats was the sire of the Cheltenham Gold Cup winner Master Oats and of the Champion Hurdle winner Flakey Dove.

Fortunately there are at the present time, two horses who have made their name whilst still alive. These are Presenting and Old Vic. The first named horse, who ran third in the Derby, is the sire of the Gold Cup winners Denman and War Of Attrition. Old Vic, who won both the French and Irish Derbies, failed to make the grade as a sire on the Flat, but was to find his niche as a jumping sire, being the progenitor of the Grand National winner Comply Or Die as well as the Gold Cup winner Kicking King – the latter also being the winner of two runnings of the King George VI Chase.

In the formative years of steeplechasing it was the sires Melbourne (see *The Godolphin Arabian*) and Hermit who laid the foundations of English jumping blood – the first named being the ancestor of My Prince. But the direct lines of both horses have died out and while steeplechasing owes them a great debt, their names have no practical significance at the present time.

In the years following the war four stallions who exerted a strong jumping influence were My Prince, Cottage, Fortina and Vulgan. My Prince sired the Grand National winners Reynoldstown (who won the race twice) Gregalach and Royal Mail, as well as the Gold Cup winners Prince Regent and Easter Hero. Cottage was the sire of Grand National winners Lovely Cottage, Sheila's Cottage and Workman in addition to Cottage Rake, who won the Gold Cup three times. Vulgan sired the Grand National winners Team Spirit, Gay Trip and Foinavon; The Dikler, the

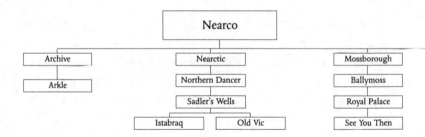

winner of the Gold Cup, and the Champion Hurdle winner Salmon Spray. Fortina, the winner of the Gold Cup and one of the few jumping "entires", sired two Gold Cup winners in Fort Leney and Glencaraig Lady.

Outstanding amongst the jumping sires in the period immediately preceding the present decade were Deep Run, The Parson and Strong Gale. Deep Run's daughter Dawn Run was the only horse to win both the Champion Hurdle and the Gold Cup and Deep Run was responsible for two further Champion Hurdle winners in the own-brothers Morley Street and Granville Again. The Parson sired Killone Abbey and Brittany Boy, the winners respectively of the Scottish and Irish Grand Nationals. The numerous winners sired by Strong Gale included the Irish Grand National winner Feathered Gale.

The male line of Nearco, predominant in Flat racing, has equally made its presence felt in the sphere of jumping. Arkle, the winner of three Cheltenham Gold Cups and the leading chaser of the post-war period was a grandson of Nearco through the latter's son Archive, an indifferent but beautifully bred racehorse. The triple Champion Hurdle winners See You Then and Istabraq also belong to the Nearco male line – the first through Mossborough, Ballymoss and Royal Palace; the latter as a son of Sadler's Wells. The last-named horse is, incidentally, the sire of Old Vic and of other good jumping sires, including Accordion (now dead) and Oscar.

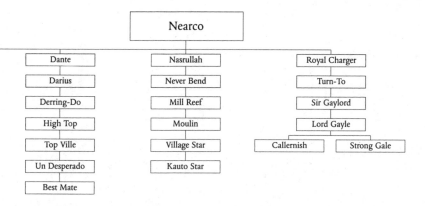

Other Northern Dancer line horses to make their mark in jump racing are the Champion Hurdle winners Collier Bay and Punjabi.

The ill-fated Best Mate, who won three Gold Cups, comes down from Nearco, through Derring-Do (*see Dante*) High Top, Top Ville and Un Desperado.

Strong Gale also belongs to the Nearco male line, whilst Callernish (who shares the same sire in Lord Gayle) sired the Cheltenham Gold Cup winner Imperial Call. The male line of Nearco's son Nasrullah is represented by the outstanding French import Kauto Star, twice the winner of the Gold Cup and three times the winner of the King George VI Chase, and by the Champion Hurdle winner Rooster Booster.

Other Nearco male line horses to win the Grand National are Amberleigh House, Numbersixvalverde, Mon Mome and Red Marauder.

The line of Prince Chevalier (St. Simon line) is extinct in terms of top-class Flat racing, but influential in racing over obstacles. He is the grandsire (through Pampered King) of Deep Run (*see over*). David Jack, also by Pampered King, sired the Gold Cup winner Davy Lad. Pirate King, a brother to Pampered King, was the grandsire of the Gold Cup winner Garrison Savannah. Court Harwell, a further Prince Chevalier horse, was the grandsire of the Gold Cup winner Master Smudge and of the Grand National winners Aldaniti and Corbiere (*see over*).

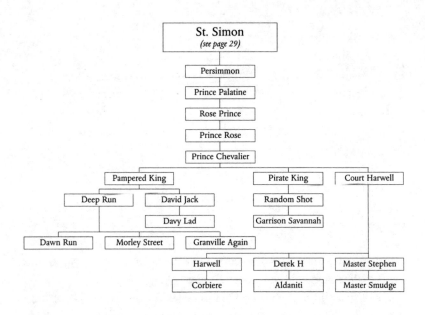

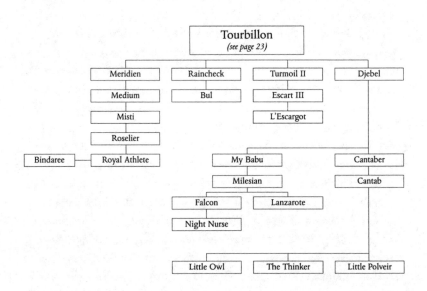

The line of Tourbillon has made its mark on jump racing. Raincheck, a son of Tourbillon sired the dual Champion Hurdle winner Bula. Escart III, a grandson of Tourbillon, was responsible for L'Escargot, the winner of two Gold Cups and of the Grand National. Djebel was the ancestor of dual Champion Hurdle winner Night Nurse, of a further Champion Hurdle winner in Lanzarote, of the Grand National winner Little Polveir and of the Gold Cup winners Little Owl and The Thinker. The Grand National winners Royal Athlete and Bindaree are by Tourbillon's descendant Roselier, who was unmatched as a sire of staying chasers.

Hyperion (see over), the grandsire of The Parson, was also the grandsire of the Grand National winners Sundew and Anglo. Other descendants of Hyperion to have won the Grand National are Lucius, Ben Nevis, Maori Venture, Party Politics, Miinnehoma and Lord Gyllene. Silver Buck, a great grandson of Hyperion, won the Gold Cup in addition to three runnings of the King George VI Chase.

Other descendants of Hyperion to make their mark in jumping are the dual Champion Hurdle winner Hardy Eustace and a further Champion Hurdle winner in Make A Stand.

Busted (see Blandford line) has made the presence of his sire line felt as the progenitor of Crash Course (see earlier) and the grandsire of Presenting. Bustineto and Clearly Bust, two further sons of Busted, are the sires of the Grand National winners Bobbyjo and Silver Birch respectively.

Montelimar, a great grandson of Ribot, has sired the Grand National winners Monty's Pass and Hedgehunter. The Cheltenham Gold Cup winners Mr Mulligan and See More Business are also representatives of the Ribot male line.

One of the outstanding chasers of the post-war years was Desert Orchid, who in addition to winning the Gold Cup and the Irish Grand National, won an unprecedented four runnings of the valuable King George VI Chase. Desert Orchid hailed from the male line of Fairway and came down through Fair Trial, Court Martial, Major Portion, Double-U-Jay and Grey Mirage.

The National Stud at Newmarket adopted the policy of standing, or

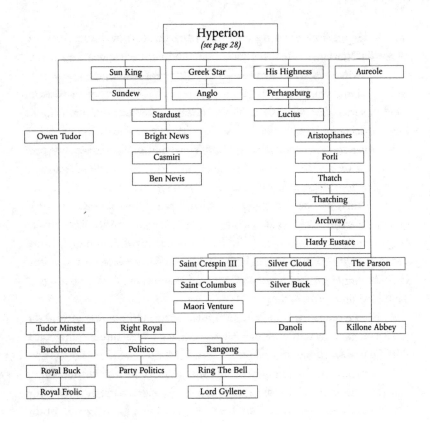

managing, potential jumping stallions as well as top-class Flat racehorses. The first "National Hunt" stallion to come under their management was Relkino, who ran second in the Derby but was a disappointment as a sire of winners on the Flat. He made his mark as a sire of performers over obstacles, his jumping progeny including Relkeel, one the leading hurdlers in training in his day.

A jumper does not need to be jumping bred on both sides of his pedigree. A measure of speed is essential in a jumper; but it is a waste of time and money to try to breed good jumpers from anything but mares and sires of reasonably good bone and build. The late John Hislop considered that it was preferable to introduce speed through the dam, citing the instance of Prince Regent, whose dam was an own-sister to the smart sprinter Diomedes. Today, however, relatively few mares in this category will be bred to jumping stallions. For an own-sister to a high-class sprinter will be looked upon favourably by the connections of a high-class sire on the Flat; and the owner of a mare with a top-class sprinting pedigree is likely to prefer the prospect of a quicker return through breeding a commercial yearling than the longer term prospect of breeding a jumper.

In the majority of jumping pedigrees today it will be the sire who provides the class and the speed – while the mare is likely to be less fashionably bred. Deep Run possessed no small amount of speed, being one of the leading two-year-olds of his year, although he was capable of winning over a mile and a half. The Parson broke down in training before he had had time to prove himself on the racecourse. But being a son of Aureole and a mare who is closely related to a St Leger winner, his pedigree did represent classic blood.

Good racehorses on the Flat who fail to meet the demands of the commercial breeders (examples being many winners of the St Leger and Ascot Gold Cup – races which are "out of fashion") often possess the qualities which jumping breeders hold in high esteem – stamina, substance, soundness and bone. Horses of this type are becoming increasingly popular as jumping sires, whilst the Derby winner Henbit is an example of a horse who failed as a sire on the Flat but made good as a sire of jumpers, his progeny including the Champion Hurdle winner Kribensis.

There are some instances of jumping pedigrees which are hard to account for. Red Rum, the only horse in history to have won the Grand National three times, possessed a pedigree which barely entitled him to stay a mile on the Flat. (He was by the miler Quorum out of a mare by the sprinter Magic Red.) On the Flat Red Rum never won beyond seven furlongs, but there is no doubt that he was more than equal to the challenge of the world's toughest steeplechase. (It is also worth mentioning in passing that Magic Red was the sire of the Grand National winner Red Alligator.) But it is the exception rather than the rule for horses bred on a purely sprinting pattern to win the principal contests over obstacles.

It is appropriate at this point to mention two jumping families who were "promoted" to the *General Stud Book* from the Non-Thoroughbred Register. Easter Hero traced to an Arab mare who performed in a circus, and was therefore not eligible for the *GSB* under the terms then in force. The family however has since been promoted, and two of its members, Morley Street and Granville Again, justified the family's promotion by winning the Champion Hurdle.

Another family of non-thoroughbred origin which has made an impact on jumping is that known as the "Drumcree" family (an earlier member of the family of that name had won the Grand National). Prominent members of the family include Tiberetta, who was in the frame in three successive Grand Nationals, Royal Relief, winner of the Champion Chase at Cheltenham, Spanish Steps, winner of the Hennessy Gold Cup, Riverside Boy, winner of the Welsh Grand National and Red Marauder, the winner of the Aintree Grand National. These families are now recognised as thoroughbred. But purity of the blood does not seem essential in a jumper; conformation, size and substance are more important than pedigree. A badly made horse, lacking in substance, may win a good race on the Flat, but it will never carry twelve stone over fences or hurdles.

It is not easy to pass judgement on the subject of inbreeding or outcrossing of jumpers. But bearing in mind the work that a jumper has to carry out, an outbred horse is more likely to be suitable than an in-bred one. It is true that Anglo, the winner of the 1966 Grand National, was inbred 2x3 to Hyperion. But it is unlikely that the obtaining of a double cross of the Derby winner was the objective of the breeder of Anglo when he planned the mating. In any aspect of jumping the practical is more important than the theoretical, and this equally applies to breeding. Lines of blood can provide a useful guideline but no more. They should not be given precedence over soundness, conformation or performance.

CHAPTER 12:

FRENCH SADDLE-BREDS

The appellation A.Q.P.S. (*Autre Que Pur Sang*, which, translated, means Non Thoroughbred) may appear to be out of place in a work whose title suggests that it is concerned with the purity of the blood. But the last 20 years have seen the emergence of a breed of horses who answer to this description and who are exerting a major influence in steeplechases and hurdle races not only in their native France, but also increasingly in Great Britain. For this reason, combined with the fact that the thoroughbred remains the dominant influence in their pedigrees, it is imperative to include them in any volume concerning the modern racehorse.

Many of the French non-thoroughbred horse population are so described for the same reason as similarly bred horses in Great Britain and Ireland. They are ineligible for the stud books of any recognised Turf Authority because their pedigrees cannot be traced according to the requirements of that authority. It is a different matter however with horses answering the description of "Selle Français", or French Saddle-Bred, a breed which has evolved from selective outcrossing with non-thoroughbreds.

In addition to steeplechasing and hurdling, Saddle-Breds are often aimed at other sports, such as trotting, eventing and showjumping. They are barred from racing against thoroughbreds on the Flat in France and can only run in Flat events confined to non-thoroughbreds. The dams of "Selle Français" winners are not listed in *Meres de Gagnants*, the volume which records the dams of any winner under Rules in France. This is in contrast to Great Britain and Ireland where all mares who have bred

Flat-race winners under any recognised rules are included in the *Statistical Record* or *Keylock's Dams of Winners*, regardless of their thoroughbred or non-thoroughbred status.

The horse who has done more than any other to publicise the "Selle Francais" breed is The Fellow. The winner of the Cheltenham Gold Cup at the fourth attempt in 1994, he also scored two victories in the King George VI Chase. Nupsala, from the same stable as The Fellow, had struck the first blow for the French saddle-bred when winning the Kempton race in 1987 whilst a third horse from the same yard, Algan, made it four in the 1994 running of the race.

There does not appear to be any set formula for the "purpose-breeding" involved. The non-thoroughbred element in the pedigree may be introduced through either the sire or the dam. In the case of The Fellow the "impure" element in the pedigree comes through the sire Italic (also the sire of Antonin, winner of the Ritz Club Chase at Cheltenham); L'Oranaise, the dam of The Fellow, is a thoroughbred. Italic won minor races on the Flat open to non-thoroughbreds up to eleven furlongs and went on to win six races over fences. Although not clean-bred, he belongs to a male line in the Stud Book, being by Carnaval, by Fast Fox, by Fastnet, by Pharos, by Phalaris. L'Oranaise was unraced. She also bred Al Capone II, an own-brother to The Fellow, who was one of France's top steeplechasers, Quick Fellow, an additional own-brother to the above pair and L'Oran (by Mondain).

However the majority of the most successful saddle-breds are by thoroughbred sires and inherit the non-thoroughbred element through their dams. Nupsala is a son of the TB Laniste, a good-class performer on the Flat at around a mile and a quarter. (Laniste is by Tarquin, by Scratch II, by Pharis II, by Pharos). The dam of Nupsala is Upsala III, a winner on the Flat and of twelve jumping races; Upsala III also bred Judy, whose son Uccello II won the Grand Steeplechase de Paris, France's most important event over the bigger obstacles. Upsala III is by Verdi (TB) out of Lakme (SF).

French-saddle breds continue to make their presence felt over fences in the UK. First Gold was the winner of the King George VI Chase;

Mon Mome won the Grand National; and Azertyuiop the Queen Mother Chase.

First Gold is a son of Shafoun, a winner of the French Champion Hurdle, who is by Labus, by Busted. The dam of First Gold, Nuit D'Or, a high-class cross-country performer, was sired by the TB Pot D'Or, the winner of the Grand Steeplechase de Paris. The next dam was the "Selle Français" mare Fynole.

Mon Mome is by Passing Sale, by No Pass No Sale, by Northfields, by Northern Dancer. His non-thoroughbred dam, Etoile Du Lion (by Target), won over ten furlongs on the Flat in France.

Valfinet did much to advertise the value of French saddle-breds over the smaller obstacles. A dual winner of the Kingwell Hurdle at Wincanton, he is by the TB sire Maiymad (also the sire of the French Champion Hurdle winner Ubu III). Maiymad, a useful performer on the Flat, is by Rheingold, by Faberge II, by Princely Gift, by Nasrullah. The dam of Valfinet is the saddle-bred mare Olad, a winner on the Flat and over jumps in France.

A French saddle-bred who was even more successful in the field of hurdling was Hors La Loi III, the winner of the Champion Hurdle. Hors La Loi III is an own-brother to the very high-class jumper Cyborgo, who won at the Cheltenham Festival. Cyborg, the sire of these two horses, is by Arctic Tern, by Sea-Bird. The non-thoroughbred in the pedigree is Quintessence, the dam of Hors La Loi III and Cyborgo. She was a winner on the Flat and over jumps.

The emergence of the French saddle-bred horse has served to reinforce the point that purity of the blood is less important in a jumper than the correct conformation. It is, however, also evident that retaining a preponderance of thoroughbred blood remains a major objective.

CONCLUSION

The appraisal of pedigrees is essentially a personal matter. It is possible to argue indefinitely on the merits and demerits of bloodlines and families. Many people take dislikes to certain horses or certain bloodlines for no discernible reason other than the holding of prejudices which they cannot put into words.

Many stallions who possessed top-class ability on the racecourse fail to become popular with breeders through faulty conformation or through possessing an unfashionable pedigree. Equally many classic winners of no more than average ability receive good support from breeders on the grounds of an illustrious ancestry and good conformation.

Young sires whose first crop of yearlings are in strong demand can soon fall from favour if their progeny fail to make their mark on the racecourse. Other stallions who start their stud life at a low fee can soon become fashionable if they sire a high percentage of winners.

It is possible to form a shrewd idea of which stallions will succeed at stud; but it is not possible to predict the outcome of their careers with any certainty. Breeding is an inexact science and it is impossible to be dogmatic on the subject. But some form of constructive advice is essential to the beginning breeder if he is to increase his chances of success.

It is to be hoped that the layman now realises that the apparently daunting words in the terminology of thoroughbred breeding are simple when analysed and were not devised to puzzle him!

A GUIDE TO FURTHER READING

The history of the thoroughbred is a very large subject indeed. And it is not possible in a work of this nature to give this subject more than the barest of outlines. The books listed below are recommended for further reading. The list is not comprehensive, but all the books mentioned are informative or entertaining, and in many cases both these things.

The person who wishes to purchase all these works will find himself or herself faced with a large financial outlay. It is however possible to have access to these books without buying them. The Thoroughbred Breeders' Association, Stanstead House, The Avenue, Newmarket, Suffolk CB8 9AA (Tel. 01638-661321) has an extensive library of books to which all members can refer.

REFERENCE BOOKS AND PERIODICALS

Bloodstock Sales Review, Weatherbys Group Limited, Sanders Road, Wellingborough, Northants NN8 4BX. Tel: 01933 440077

Directory Of The Turf, P.O. Box 7677, Hungerford, Berks RG17 0FX. Tel: 01488 684321

European Pattern Book, Weatherbys Group Limited, as above.

General Stud Book, Weatherbys Group Limited, as above

Irish Field Directory, Irish Field, Irish Farm Centre, Bluebell, Dublin 12

James Underwood's European Racing & Breeding Digest, 94 Cornwall Gardens, London SW7 4AX. Tel: 020 7589 0625

Keylock's Dams Of Winners, Keylock's Publications, The Old Rectory, Lidgate, Newmarket, Suffolk CB8 9PY. Tel: 01638 50015

Thoroughbred Owner & Breeder (incorporating *Pacemaker*), Editorial, First Floor, 65 the Broadway, Haywards Heath, West Sussex RH16 3AS. Tel: 01444 440540

Pedigrees of Leading Winners 1912–1959, compiled by Franklin Birch

Pedigrees of Leading Winners 1960–1980, compiled by Michael Ross & Martin Pickering.

Racehorses, Timeform, Timeform House, Northgate, Halifax HX1 1KF. Tel: 01422 330330

Register of Non Thoroughbred Horses, Weatherbys Group Limited, as above.
Return Of Mares, Weatherbys Group Limited, as previous page.
Stallion Book, Weatherbys Group Limited, as previous page.
Statistical Record, Weatherbys Group Limited, as previous page.

RECOMMENDED BOOKS

Bloodstock Breeders' Review., Sagittarius Bloodstock Agency, The Manor
  House, Church Lane, Sproxton, Melton Mowbray, Leics LE14 4PZ.
Bloodstock Breeding, Sir Charles Leicester. Revised in 1983 by Howard
  Wright.
The Breed of the Racehorse, Friedrich Becker.
Breeding For Racing, John Hislop.
British Bloodlines, C F Jerdein and R Kaye.
The Classic Connection, Peter Pryor.
The Classic Pedigree, Michael Church.
Encyclopaedia of British Flat Racing. Peter Willett, Roger Mortimer and
  Richard Onslow.
Flat Racing, The Lonsdale Library.
The History of the British Turf, 6 vols by Sir Theodore Cook. 2
  supplementary volumes by Captain T.H. Browne.
Horse Racing, Denis Craig.
An introduction to the Thoroughbred, Peter Willett.
Makers of the Modern Thoroughbred, Peter Willett.
Thoroughbred Breeding, Mordaunt Milner.
Thoroughbred Racing Stock, Lady Wentworth

PEDIGREE SUPPLIERS

ABI Thoroughbreds, 29 Paddocks Drive, Newmarket,
Suffolk CB8 9BE

Alan Yuill Walker, Neville House, Kintbury, Hungerford,
Berks RG17 9TJ

BBA UK Ltd, 16 Black Bear Court, Newmarket, Suffolk CB8 9AF, UK

Brain International Ltd, Hope House, 5 Cadogan Park, Woodstock,
Oxon OX20 1UW

Caballus Equine Consultancy, 52 Purley Road, Cirencester, Glos
GL7 1EP

Ian M. Deane, 74 Stevens House, Jerome Place, Kingston upon Thames,
Surrey KT1 1HX

Keylock's Publications, The Old Rectory, Lidgate, Newmarket,
Suffolk CB8 9PY

Michael Church, 134 Old Woking Road, Woking, Surrey GU22 8NY

Otterswick Marketing, PO Box 8110, Mauchline, Ayrshire KA5 5YB

Patterns and Profiles, 5 Portland Street, Lancaster LA1 1SZ

Vivian Pratt, 6 Cobbold Road, Felixstowe, Suffolk IP11 7HQ

Sagittarius Bloodstock Agency, The Manor House, Church Lane,
Sproxton, Melton Mowbray, Leics LE14 4PZ

Thoroughbred Genetics Ltd, Godmersham Park, Godmersham,
Canterbury, Kent CT4 7DT

Vivian Pratt, 6 Cobbold Road, Felixstowe, Suffolk IP11 7HQ

Weatherbys Bloodstock Reports, Weatherbys Group Ltd, Sanders Road,
Wellingborough, Northants NN8 4BX

Welsh Bloodstock, 45 Heritage Park, Haverfordwest, Pembrokeshire
SA61 2QF

BOOKSELLERS
The market for books on bloodstock breeding is comparatively restricted. Most booksellers, therefore, do not stock breeding books of the more specialist kind.

There are, however, a small number of organisations whose list of bloodstock and racing titles, both new and second hand, is extensive. They are listed below.

Classic Racing Books
64 Stephens Way
Bignall End
Stoke-On-Trent
Staffs ST7 8NL
Tel (01882) 722394
Stockists of books on all aspects of racing and breeding both new and second hand as well as Timeform Annuals.

The Marlborough Bookshop & Gallery
Weston-Super-Mare
Somerset
Tel: (01934) 613996
One of the leading suppliers of racing books new and second hand & racing prints for a world-wide clientele.

Racecourse & Covertside
14 Clinton Avenue
Hampton Magna
Warks CV35 8TX
Tel (01926) 495712
This firm supplies books on all aspects of racing, field sports and general horse, both new and second hand. They exhibit on many racecourses.

Raceform
High Street
Compton, Newbury
Berks RG20 6NL
Tel: 01933 304858
Web: www.racingpost.com/shop
Publisher and bookseller stocking a wide range of racing publications.

Tindalls Booksellers
54–56 High Street
Newmarket
Suffolk CB8 8LE
Tel: 01638 561760
Fax: 01638 561782

R.E. & G.B. Way
Brettons
Burrough Green
Newmarket
Suffolk CB8 9NA
Tel: 01638 507217
Website: www.way-books.co.uk
Antiquarian & second hand booksellers.

Weatherbys Bookshop
Sanders Road
Wellingborough
Northants NN8 4BX
Tel: 01933 440077
Fax: 01933 270370
Website: www.weatherbys-bookshop.com
Weatherbys Bookshop stocks a wide range of racing and general
equestrian publications along with racing videos.

GLOSSARY

The following words and phrases are all in common use in the parlance of thoroughbred breeding. Some have appeared in the text, although without adequate explanation; others have not.

A.Q.P.S. "Autre Que Pur Sang" – an appellation referring to French horses purpose-bred mainly for steeplechasing and hurdling.

Black Type Races. Horses who have won or been placed in Pattern or Listed races are recorded in sales catalogues in black type. Hence the term "black type race" is used with reference to races in this category.

Bloodlines. Male or female lines of descent.

Blood Nicks. A nick is said to occur when two lines of blood consistently produce better results when mated together than when mated elsewhere.

Bloodstock Agencies. These agencies buy and sell bloodstock of all categories both at home and abroad. They will either arrange private deals between buyers and vendors or they will bid on a client's behalf at public auctions. Agencies also compile pedigrees, syndicate and promote stallions and arrange shipping and insurance.

Bottom Line. Line of female descent.

Brothers and Sisters and other relationships. Brothers and Sisters are known as Full Brothers and Sisters or Own-Brothers and Sisters. Horses who are by the same sire and out of the same dam. Sadler's Wells and Fairy King were own-brothers since they were both by Northern Dancer out of Fairy Bridge.

Half Brothers and Sisters are out of the same dam but by a different sire. Thus Nashwan, by Blushing Groom out of Height of Fashion, was a half-brother to Unfuwain, by Northern Dancer out of Height of Fashion.

Three Quarter Brothers and Sisters or Three Parts Brothers and Sisters who are out of the same dam and have as their sires animals who were half-brothers in the sense described above or were by the same sire but out of a different dam. Thus the Prix de l'Arc de Triomphe winner Saumarez, by Rainbow Quest by Blushing Groom out of Fiesta Fun was a three-parts a brother to Balliol Boy, by Nashwan by Blushing Groom out of Fiesta Fun.

Classic Races. In England the classic races are the 2000 Guineas, Derby and St. Leger for three-year-old colts and fillies and the 1000 Guineas and Oaks for three-year-old fillies only. The classic races in Ireland correspond to those in England, except that the Irish St. Leger is open to older horses.

The races in France which correspond to the English classics are the Poule d'Essai des Poulains (2000 Guineas), Poule d'Essai des Pouliches (1000 Guineas), Prix du Jockey Club (Derby), Prix de Diane (Oaks) and Prix Royal-Oak (St Leger). The last named race is also open to older horses. In addition the Grand Prix de Paris is staged for colts and fillies.

In America, the three races which constitute the "Triple Crown" are the Kentucky Derby, the Preakness Stakes and the Belmont Stakes.

Commercial Breeding. Breeding with the sales ring as the principal objective rather than to produce a good racehorse.

Families. Lines of female descent.

Fertility. On an average about 70% of all mares covered each season conceive. But conception does not ensure that the mare will produce a live and healthy foal. Miscarriages and deaths of foals reduce the average of surviving foals to about 65% of mares covered.

Half-Bred. A non-thoroughbred horse, i.e. a horse who is ineligible to be entered in the General Stud Book.

Inbreeding. The mating of closely related animals.

Linebreeding. A less intensive form of inbreeding.

Listed Race. A race of importance below the grade of Pattern race.

Pattern Races. Prestige events. In 1966 a Committee was set up under the chairmanship of the late Duke of Norfolk to examine the Pattern of Racing. The Committee recommended that "over the correct distances and at the correct times of year, races should be available to test the best horses of all ages." They designated 100 races to receive added money. These races became known as "Pattern Races." These races are now framed on an internationally agreed format and are divided into Groups 1, 2, or 3 according to the level of prize money which is allotted to them.

Syndication of Stallions. It was formerly the practice with the most successful racehorses when they commenced stud duties to capitalise them into 60 shares – sixty mares then being the number that a top-class stallion would cover during the course of a stud season. Each share sold then entitled the breeder/shareholder to one nomination annually for the remainder of that horses's stud life. If a breeder did not wish to use his nomination during any particular stud season, he had the right to sell this nomination to another breeder for a privately agreed sum.

During the last two decades this system has undergone many changes. A top-class stallion will now serve a book of 150 or more mares during a stud season.

Tail Female Line. Direct line of female descent.

Thoroughbred. A horse who is entered in or eligible to be entered in the *General Stud Book.*

Triple Crown. When a colt wins all three of the classic races (i.e. the 2000 Guineas, the Derby and the St. Leger) he is described as having won the "Triple Crown". The "Fillies' Triple Crown" races are the 1000 Guineas, Oaks and St. Leger. When a horse is described as having won the "American Triple Crown" this means that he is the winner of all the three American classics (i.e. the Preakness Stakes, the Kentucky Derby and the Belmont Stakes).